made at a previous meeting) and disguise themselves as men. During their rehearsal for the Assembly (which they plan to attend illegally), Praxagora proves to be the only one capable of speaking in the appropriate manner. She makes a practice speech that points out the defects of the present democracy— Athenians use the Assembly too much, pay people for attending, are swayed by worthless men, are fickle and lack unity—but she does not yet say much that is communistic. Most importantly, she proposes that the city be turned over to the women, "for in fact we use them as administrators and treasurers in our households" (211–12).

The actual goings-on at the Assembly are not part of the play. We glean what happens there from things said at the rehearsal and, most importantly, from discussions that occur after the Assembly takes place. Chremes tells Blepyrus, the husband of Praxagora, that the Assembly was packed with a lot of pale-faced men (the women, of course), and because there was such a large crowd, a lot of regulars did not get in (and, more importantly, did not receive their pay for attending). The women received some opposition, but in the end they were victorious: the Assembly voted to turn the city over to the women.

We learn of Praxagora's communistic program in a discussion she has with Blepyrus. When Blepyrus tells Praxagora that rule has been handed over to the women, Praxagora (acting surprised, for she cannot betray the conspiracy) expresses her delight, for there will no longer be false witnesses, informers, theft, envy, poverty, or quarreling. Asked why, she presents her communistic views and begins by advocating a community of property:

I assert that it is necessary for everyone to share and have everything in common and to live the same, and not for one to be rich while another is miserable, nor for one to farm much land while to another there isn't enough to bury himself, nor to possess many slaves while another doesn't even possess an attendant. But I make one way of life common to all. . . . I'll make the land common for all, and the silver and anything else that is held individually. Then, from these common things we will maintain you, dispensing and saving and attending to you. (590–94, 599–600)

Blepyrus asks, quite sensibly, why anyone would lay down his possessions for everyone to have in common instead of holding on to his goods. What about self-interest or dishonesty? Praxagora replies:

No one will do anything because of poverty, for everyone will have everything: cakes, slices of salt fish, barley loaves, clothing, wine, garlands, and chickpeas. So what would be the advantage in not laying down what one has? (605–607)

Blepyrus objects to the communism of property, because property, he says, is needed to win the favors of girls. Although his response is shallow, he (as well as Aristophanes) recognizes that not all advantages are economic ones, thereby making the communism of property imperfect. In other words, to make all people equal, or to make them all equally happy, one must do more than simply give everyone an equal share of goods. Praxagora's reply brings us to the communism of women: a man will be able to sleep with a girl free of charge. "For I'm making women common to men to lie with, and to make children with (for those who want to)" (613–15). But Blepyrus replies: "Then won't everyone go after the girl who is in fullest bloom . . . ?" (615–16). Blepyrus intends to hold Praxagora to her promise of full equality. He complains that everyone will want the best-looking men and women. There will be long lines for the beautiful people, but who will want to spend time with the old and the ugly? It is surely not a state of equality for the ugly and old always to have to stand in long lines, and yet never to have long lines waiting for them. Agreeing that this is wrong, Praxagora offers the following solution: "The sorriest and most snub-nosed girls will sit down beside the majestic ones, and if he lusts after the latter, he must first bang the ugly one" (617–18). And similarly, "it will not be possible for women to sleep with the handsome and well-built men until they grant their favors to the ugly and small ones" (628–29). The unequal advantage that some people have of being desirable is eliminated by making the desirable and the undesirable as equal as possible. Praxagora says that this "proposal is democratic, and it will be a great mockery of the most majestic . . ." (631–32).

Blepyrus next asks how each of us will be able to distinguish his own child. Praxagora replies that this will not be necessary, because everyone will consider every man who is older (within a certain range of ages) to be his father. Blepyrus is afraid that this will lead to impious crimes (e.g., the assault of one's father) due to ignorance of who one's real father is. But Praxagora claims the opposite is true: Whereas normally people do not care about anyone but themselves and their own, under her communism of children, everyone will come to the rescue of any older man who is being assaulted, for fear that he might be their real father.

Having described the communism of property, women, and children, Praxagora finishes by tying up some loose ends.

13

Land will be farmed by slaves. There will be no theft or civil suits, because these involve the desire to gain property, and why should someone attempt to acquire what is already (in a sense) theirs? Assault will be punished through the exclusion from meals. She also describes the further transformation of the city into one big family or household. For example, law courts, which will no longer have a function, will be turned into large dining rooms for the common meals.

Aristophanes next moves to Praxagora's communism in practice. He presents two scenes that serve to illustrate how her theory will work (or rather, fail to work): The first centers on a man named Chremes (730–876), a law-abiding citizen—in fact, he's a bit too law-abiding: He is overly optimistic and gullible, and he earlier agreed with Praxagora's plan (without raising an eyebrow). The scene begins with Chremes preparing his goods to be given to the city so that they can be used in common. He is confronted by a man who is not going to give away his hard-earned property until he sees what the rest of the city does. Chremes, he says, is a fool for doing otherwise: It is in the nature of people to take, not to give—and if Chremes is stupid enough to give away his property, you can be sure, the man says, that there will be people eager to take it, leaving Chremes with nothing. Besides, the Athenians are fickle. Who is to say something won't happen to change the Assembly's decree, thus abolishing communism of property? Then where would Chremes be?

Toward the end of this scene, a heraldess tempts people to turn in their goods by announcing a feast for all those who comply with the ruling of the Assembly. When the man hears this, he tries to find some clever scheme to attend the feast without giving up his goods.

Aristophanes moves abruptly to the next scene, which involves a young man, a girl, and three hags (877–1111). This scene is in a sense the climax of the play. Here, we find a beautiful girl and an old hag, both apparently waiting for something. Unbeknownst to the girl, they are both waiting for the girl's handsome lover. When the youth finally arrives, the hag convinces him that according to the law, he must sleep with her before he can lie with the girl. The girl, quite illegally, fights with the hag, who runs off. A second, even uglier hag appears. She wants the lover. But a third hag—with a face like a monkey—arrives; she wants him, too. The second hag claims the youth, but the third hag replies that, on the contrary, he must come with her, because she is uglier than the second. In the name of equality, the law must favor the ugliest. The scene ends with the two hags engaged in a tug of war over the bewildered young lover. Misery is not abolished, it is merely redistributed.

Despite the sad consequences of Praxagora's plan, the play ends on a happy note with a grand banquet (1112–83). There's a happy man and a happy maid, plenty of wine and dancing girls, and a fantastic meal. All the physical pleasures are fulfilled: sex with anyone, a meal made of everything, and so on. This, after all, is the aim of Praxagora's communism, or at least it is all that can be expected. Anything nobler has been leveled.

2. THE AIM OF THE
ASSEMBLY OF WOMEN

At the end of the play, the chorus or chorus leader says to the audience: "I want to make a small suggestion to the judges: To the wise ones, remember to judge me victor for my wisdom, while to the ones who laugh pleasantly, remember to judge me victor because of the laughter" (1154–56). On one level, Aristophanes' aims are quite obvious: He wants to make the audience laugh (this is comedy, after all), and he wants to win the competition the play was entered in.[3] But, as the passage just quoted suggests, Aristophanes most likely had other intentions besides these. (As the chorus in the *Frogs* says, "grant me to say much that is funny, but also much that is serious" [389–90].) Aristophanes was also appealing to the wisdom of the wise, i.e., he wanted his audience (or parts of it, anyway) to think. And he does make us think. For the *Assembly of Women* is a critique of contemporary politics (e.g., political figures and trends), and, more fundamentally, a critique of a particular philosophical outlook, namely communism (and the conception of justice inherent in it).

It is certainly the case that the *Assembly of Women* speaks to the political issues of the day (though it is unclear what that "day" is—scholars generally date the play to 393, 392, or 391[4]). Aristophanes seems to praise moderate democrats like Myrionides—from the "good ol' days"—and Thrasybulus, and he attacks radical democrats like Epicrates, Agyrrhius, and Cephalus. He was especially opposed to Agyrrhius's institution of pay for attending the Assembly (and his later raising of the pay from one and then two to three obols).[5]

16

However important these issues were to Aristophanes and his audience, I am going to pass over them and turn to an aim of the *Assembly of Women* that I believe is more fundamental, and more interesting to modern readers: the critique of communism.[6]

Nothing—short of real life—can concretize an ethical or political theory the way literature can. This is true even of comic literature, especially if the theory one wishes to bring to life is a theory one rejects. Comedy, in fact, is an excellent vehicle for bashing those ideas with which we disagree. And this, I believe, is precisely what Aristophanes is doing in the *Assembly of Women*: He is treating a serious moral issue comically—or perhaps he would prefer to say he is treating the issue both comically and seriously at the same time. But what issue? On one level he is considering the question: How should the city be arranged? and he is rejecting the answer: Communistically. But more fundamentally (even if only implicitly) I believe Aristophanes is attacking and lampooning a certain notion of justice which lies at the foundation of the communism of the *Assembly of Women*.

Aristotle on Justice

Although Aristotle (384–322 B.C.E.) comes after Aristophanes, a brief look at his conception of justice will help us to understand what Aristophanes is up to.

According to Aristotle, there are basically two ways of understanding the concept of justice, one general and the other specific (see *Nicomachean Ethics* V.1). Justice in the general

17

sense is simply virtue in relation to others (see especially *Nico-machean Ethics* V.1.1129b30ff.). Justice in the special sense (which is included in the more general conception) is fairness (or equality, τὸ ἴσον). Aristotle discusses many forms of this sort of justice, but there are two things true of justice as fairness in all its forms: (1) Justice is getting what you deserve, merit, are worth (which depends on the context and a certain standard of what is worthy or good); (2) Justice is equal in that those who are of the same worth deserve the same goods and/or treatment, and unequal in that those who are not the same do not deserve the same goods and/or treatment. For example, according to advocates of aristocracy, all citizens with a certain high degree of practical wisdom must have access to the highest political offices (and in this sense justice demands equality), but those citizens without the requisite practical wisdom will not be allowed to hold such offices (and in this sense justice demands inequality). Justice is proportional equality. (See *Nicomachean Ethics* V.2–5, and, for a summary, V.2.1130b30ff.)

I mention Aristotle's views on justice because although his account is philosophically deeper than any that came before it, the justice he describes (both general and specific—but mostly the latter; see *Nicomachean Ethics* V.3.1131a14–27) can accurately be described as the traditional conception, which is getting what you deserve (according to your merit). I believe Aristophanes in the *Assembly of Women* is defending some form of this traditional notion of justice, and rejecting an alternative theory of justice implied in Praxagora's communistic scheme.

Justice in the Assembly of Women

I shall look first at instances of the traditional notion of jus-tice in the *Assembly of Women.*

At the opening of the play, Praxagora (in a parody of tragic speech) is speaking to a lamp as if to the sun god. She reveals the women's revolutionary plan to the lamp alone, because of the service done for women by the lamp—i.e., because the lamp alone deserves to hear it (7–18). More importantly, the women tell Praxagora she will be chosen leader if she proves to be worthy of it, i.e., if she pulls off their plan (246–47).

Praxagora's communism will be pretty much devoid of the traditional notion of justice (as we shall see), but even in the communistic city she envisions it pops up occasionally. For instance, some crimes will be punished, i.e., in some cases those who commit crimes—and only those—will be punished because they deserve to be (663–66, but cf. 668–71). In addi-tion, those who were cowards in battle will not be able to attend public dinners (679–80).

Finally, Praxagora many times in her rehearsal speech seems to appeal to the traditional notion of justice in her crit-icisms of Athenian politics: the Assembly uses worthless men but ignores worthy ones; Athenians fear those who love them but embrace those who do not (173–88, 193–203). The city must be turned over to the women, she argues, because they merit the rule more than the men do (209–40).

Since violations of this form of justice seem, in Praxagora's view, to be a cause of the city's ills, one might expect some advocacy on her part for a return to this justice. However, with the minor exceptions noted above, this is not the case.

19

Praxagora seems to defend a radically different view of justice. Implicit in Praxagora's communism is egalitarianism: justice is equality, understood strictly, not proportionally. On this view, roughly all people (that is, citizens) should have available to them the same things and live the same kind of life.

Aristotle claims that one mistake of democracy is its acceptance of the idea that justice is equality without recognizing that justice is also (in a sense) inequality (see *Politics* III.9.1280a11–24). Although Praxagora describes her scheme as popular or democratic (δημοτική, 631), her egalitarianism goes far beyond anything advocated by the radical democracy criticized by Aristotle.

As was seen when I presented the action of the play, Praxagora's egalitarianism is achieved through a communism both of property and of women. First, everyone is to share all material goods in common, and thus live a common life (590–600). But this is not enough to make all citizens equal. So, second, women are to be made common for all men (and vice versa). This will be arranged in such a way that "sexual wealth" (i.e., physical beauty) is shared in common (611–29). The beautiful and the ugly will be made equal (see 630). Finally, life will also be made common by turning the town into a single habitation (673ff.).

Aristophanes' Criticism of Egalitarian Justice

There are many implicit attacks against egalitarianism in the *Assembly of Women*. Here are the two most significant.

The first comes from the scene with Chremes, whose

point seems to be that any city characterized by a communism of property will be full of gullible fools ready to be taken, and dishonest scoundrels ready to take. Dishonesty will still exist; it will simply have to find new ways of succeeding. The end of the scene illustrates this with a (possible) injustice that represents the general injustice of Praxagora's scheme. The dishonest man who has been speaking to Chremes says:

> By Zeus, I need some cunning plan so that I'll keep my goods *and* somehow share in these common baked goods [i.e., those at the feast]. (872–74)

Aristophanes' point is that under communism there will be a tendency for people to try to receive the advantages of common property without giving anything in return. Communism promotes (in more ways than this scene illustrates, as we shall see) some people receiving more, and others less, than they deserve. Different people contribute different amounts, but still receive the same recompense. Aristophanes argues against the communism of property by pointing out that it is silly, unworkable, and obviously unjust according to the traditional notion of justice.[7] But is it obvious that the traditional notion of justice *is* best? Aristophanes would say that clearly it is, especially if you consider what Praxagora's scheme actually requires. For this we need to turn to the second criticism, which comes from the scene with the three hags.

We remember that full equality requires more than just the communism of property. Not only must citizens all receive equal amounts of goods, unequal people must actually be made equal (to the extent that that is possible). In the scene with the three hags, Aristophanes is criticizing a certain argument, which, put generally, can be stated as follows: Any positive attribute, value, or virtue is an advantage; that *some* people have such advantages implies that others are disadvantaged; this entails inequality, which in turn entails unfairness: It is unfair that some people have advantages while others are disadvantaged. Therefore, according to this argument, any advantage must be removed (for example, by the redistribution and common ownership of property), or, the advantage must be accompanied by a penalty on those who possess it and a reward or bonus for those who do not (as we saw with the three hags). Aristophanes criticizes this position by illustrating its consequences in practice. This scene (indeed, the whole play) is something of a *reductio ad absurdum*. Any theory, he seems to be saying, that could lead to such consequences *must* be wrong. And, in general, what it leads to is the punishment of those with positive attributes or virtues, and to a competition among the others, where the persons who most lack these attributes are victorious. Justice, therefore, has become getting what you do *not* deserve: Egalitarianism demands that we reward those who lack merit or worth (in some context) and penalize those who possess it. This, for the Greek mind, is absurd. Aristophanes most likely saw this as a problem with many of the communistic ideas discussed in fifth- and early-fourth-century Athens—ideas which in part prompted him to write this play.

3. ANCIENT GREEK "COMMUNISM" BEFORE ARISTOPHANES

At the beginning of *Politics* II.7, Aristotle states that "no one else [besides Plato] has been innovative concerning the community of women and children . . ." (1266a34–35). Does this mean that no one advocated, discussed, or knew of the communism of property, women, and children before Plato? Clearly not. Aristotle himself writes that some Libyans had women in common (*Politics* II.3.1262a19–21), thus showing that others knew of, and even practiced, the communism of women. Ussher (p. xix) says that Aristotle of course knew of Aristophanes' *Assembly of Women*, and that in the above-cited passage, Aristotle is only "speaking of those who have put forward opinions *peri politeias* [concerning constitutions]," and a comedy would not qualify. (This also explains Aristophanes' claim to novelty at *Assembly of Women* 578–87: He is the first *comic poet* to broach the subject of communism.) That these ideas were not original with Plato, however, does not imply that they were ordinary or commonplace during his lifetime (see *Republic* 449c and *Timaeus* 18c); but they were certainly "in the air" when Aristophanes and Plato were active.

What follows is not intended as an exhaustive account, but as a very brief (and somewhat speculative) survey of what may have contributed to communism's being part of intellectual discussion in fifth- and fourth-century Athens.

Historical Accounts

In Herodotus's *Histories* (ca. 430 B.C.E.), there are three passages describing "barbarian" tribes where Herodotus gives a neutral account of what might loosely be called the communism of women. Describing the customs of the Massagetae, he says, "Each man marries a woman, but they have [or use] them in common" (I.216). Herodotus says of the Nasamones, that "being the custom for each man to have many women, they have sexual intercourse with them in common, in a manner resembling the Massagatae . . ." (IV.172). Also, the Auseans "have sexual intercourse with their women in common, and they do not live together [as couples], but have intercourse like beasts" (IV.180).

Xanthas, who was probably a contemporary of Herodotus, and for whom only fragments have survived, states:

> The Magians [a Median tribe] have intercourse with their mothers and daughters; and it is legal to have intercourse with sisters. Women are common, not by force or secretly, but both men consent, whenever one would like to "marry" [the woman of] another.[8]

It should be noted that in the above remarks, no account was given by Herodotus or Xanthas of *why* the various tribes practiced some form of "communism," or whether it was beneficial; it was merely reported that they lived in such a manner. In the following passage, however, reasons are given for why certain tribes live communally, or why such a communal way of life might be a pattern that Greeks should follow.

Herodotus writes that the Agathyrsi, from what is now

Transylvania, "have sexual intercourse with their women in common so that they will be brothers to each other, and all being kinsmen feel neither envy nor hatred toward each other" (IV.104). As How and Wells have pointed out, "The purpose here ascribed to [this communism of women] is a piece of Greek rationalism, and a curious anticipation of Plato, *Rep.* Bk. V."[9] That is to say, tribal peoples do not get together and decide to live communally so as to remove enmity and live in peace. Tribal living is by definition (a kind of) communal living. The expansion of brotherhood and the elimination of envy and hatred are Herodotean additions.

We now have a clue as to how communistic ideas may have (at least in part) gotten into the intellectual atmosphere. Perhaps some men, pessimistic about how things were going in the Greek city-states during certain periods,[10] saw a solution to their problems in the (often overly optimistic) reports of communal bliss coming from some travelers and historians.[11]

Sparta

Let us now turn to a culture with which the Athenians were much more familiar. Sparta (better known by the ancients as Lacedaimonia) acquired, under the laws of her traditional founder, Lycurgus, a reputation for being ascetic, disciplined, militaristic, and communistic. Since Spartan institutions most likely influenced the communistic thought of fifth- and fourth-century thinkers, they should be discussed here. (We will not examine all aspects of Spartan society, only those that appear to be "communistic.")

Unfortunately, any investigation of Lycurgan Sparta is fraught with problems. First, Lycurgus himself is semilegendary, and the details of his life are something of a mystery.[12] For instance, estimates of his date of birth range from the eleventh to the eighth century B.C.E.[13] Second, there are problems with the major sources of information about Lycurgan Sparta: Herodotus does not mention anything that could really be called communistic; Xenophon is extremely pro-Sparta, and rather inaccurate at places[14]; Aristotle, although he says some things that are of interest to us, does not consider Sparta to be an example of communism in any sense; and Polybius (second century B.C.E.) and Plutarch (ca. 50–120 C.E.) are relatively late (i.e., they come well after Plato, and may have read some form of philosophical communism into their accounts). Finally, although Plutarch says Plato adopted a Spartan theory of government (*Lycurgus* III.1), Plato does not directly mention the communism of Sparta in the *Republic*.[15] But keeping these problems in mind, let us look at some possible communistic characteristics of Spartan society.

I shall begin by mentioning some features which may have been interpreted as components of a Spartan communism of property. First, as part of their asceticism, there seems to have been legislation against (or discouraging) wealth and luxury.[16] This asceticism may have been supported by an equality of land and possessions. According to Plutarch:

> Lycurgus's second, and most revolutionary, reform was his redistribution of the land. For there was dreadful inequality: many destitute people without means were congregating in the city, while wealth had poured completely into just a few hands. In order to expel arrogance, envy, crime, luxury and those yet older and more serious political afflictions, wealth

and poverty, Lycurgus persuaded the citizens to pool all the land and then redistribute it afresh. Then they would all live on equal terms with one another, with the same amount of property to support each. . . . (VIII.1–4, trans. Talbert)[17]

There is a lot of evidence for some kind of redistribution of land, although we cannot be sure it was instituted for the reasons Plutarch gives.[18] In addition, according to Xenophon, the Spartans shared a lot in common, and this may have been seen as communistic.[19]

We turn now to the communism of women and children. First, there is a lot of evidence that marriages and procreation were regulated.[20] In addition, it may have been the case that a man could share his wife with other men. According to Xenophon and Plutarch, this was allowed in order to eliminate jealousy.[21] Polybius wrote that

> among the Lacedaimonians it was a hereditary custom and quite usual for three or four men to have one wife or even more if they were brothers, the offspring being common property of all, and when a man had begotten enough children, it was honourable and quite usual for him to give his wife to one of his friends. (XII.6, trans. Paton)

F. W. Walbank remarks:

> This is our only evidence for polyandry [i.e., women having more than one husband at a time] at Sparta; but the custom is found in various parts of the world, especially where there is a shortage of women or where the men absent themselves for long periods of time. . . . The truth of P's statement has been contested; but it finds confirmation from other evidence [i.e., from Xenophon and Plutarch]. There seems therefore reason to accept P's statement; but the origin and

real significance of such polyandry is less easy to deter-
mine.[22]

Some reasons given by modern scholars for the Spartan
communism of women are: the primitive character of Spartan
institutions, economic conditions, the independent position of
women, the shortage of women due to the 466 B.C.E. earthquake,
and moral regression. I shall not say anything here about the
merits or shortcomings of any of these explanations, but it
should be noted what is *not* given as a reason: the Spartans instituted the sharing of women in order to put an end to jealousy,
strife, and so on, as Plutarch and Xenophon claimed. These two
historians most likely embellished their accounts, employing
"after-the-fact" reasoning in much the same way Herodotus did.

As the above passage from Polybius indicates, there may
have been some sense in which, or some degree to which, children were held in common. For instance, boys most likely slept
together in groups as part of their military education, instead
of in their own parents' houses. In general, Plutarch says
Spartan children belonged to the whole city, rather than to
their parents privately; but it is not clear whether he is referring to an actual communism of children, or to the very public
nature of their educational system (or both).[23]

According to Jones,

> The famous discipline of the Spartans was attributed to
> Lycurgus. It is undoubtedly very ancient fundamentally and
> has close analogies with the customs of many primitive
> warrior tribes throughout the world.[24]

The communist or communal features of Spartan society are a
part or aspect of this tribalism, just as they were in the tribes men-

tioned by Herodotus and others. The difference may have been that in the case of Sparta, the "communism" was more worked out and actually the product of some lawmaker or lawmakers.[25]

As I have indicated, it is hard to say whose accounts are accurate, and thus there is much that cannot be trusted. Most dubious, perhaps, are some of the reasons given for various communistic institutions. But popular and widespread accounts of Lycurgan Sparta, like the tales of some faraway tribes, must have influenced, and become part of, the discussion of communistic ideas.

Euripides

Moving away from historical accounts, I should next like to examine the (anti)communistic ideas of the tragedian Euripides (ca. 484–406 B.C.E).

Two fragments have come down to us revealing Euripides' interest in the question of the communism of women. The first is his play *Ino*:

> Laws concerning women have not been laid down in a fine way, for to be well off a person should have as many women [or wives] as possible . . . , so that he casts off the evil one from his home, while pleasantly preserving the noble one. But now they look to one woman, hurling great danger. For not testing other fashions, mortal men take brides into their households as ballast.[26]

The second, and more illuminating, fragment is from the *Protesilaos*. This fragment exists in a line from Clement of

29

Alexandria (2nd c. C.E.), *Stromateis* (VI.751), the whole of which should be cited: "Plato in the *Republic* said the women are common, and Euripides in the *Protesilaios* writes that 'a woman's bed should be common'" (fr. 653). These two fragments are enough to show that the idea of a communism of women was a topic important (or current) enough for Euripides to include in two of his plays.

Communistic ideas were part of the intellectual atmosphere when Aristophanes wrote the *Assembly of Women*, and he is no doubt criticizing them. But what of the most famous ancient advocate of the communism of women, children, and property, Plato (in the *Republic*)? Was the *Republic* an object of Aristophanes' attack? Or was it in some sense a reaction to it?

4. THE ASSEMBLY OF WOMEN AND PLATO'S REPUBLIC

There is a great deal of literature on this issue, much of which is redundant. For the most part I rely on Adam's discussion in the appendix to Book V of his edition of the *Republic*.[27] His treatment of the subject is, for many reasons (not the least of which is its brevity), best. Adam, writing over ninety years ago, said that although some respected scholars reject any connection between the two works, most hold that there is a connection of some kind. This still holds true today.

Adam goes through the four kinds of evidence that have been offered in favor of the various opinions: The first is "alleged external evidence" (p. 346). This includes the claim by Aristotle that no one else but Plato has been innovative with regard to the community of women and children, and Plato's claim in the *Timaeus* that the communism of the *Republic* is strange and new. It has been argued from these passages that the *Republic* must have been written before the *Assembly of Women*. Similarly, Aristophanes' claim to novelty in the *Assembly of Women* has been used as support for the view that his work is earlier than the *Republic*. But as Adam argues, all of this is useless for the present question. (His reasons are similar to those I gave at the beginning of Part 3 of this introduction.)

The second type of evidence is "alleged or prima facie allusions either (a) to Plato in the *Assembly of Women*, or (b) to Aristophanes in the fifth book of the *Republic*" (pp. 346–50). As for (a), neither Socrates' nor Plato's name is mentioned in the *Assembly of Women*; and the so-called allusions to the *Republic* that some have claimed to find are flimsy, to say the least. As for (b), some claim Plato makes frequent reference to the *Assembly of Women* (though there is no direct mention made of it). Adam lists nine passages in the *Republic*, three of which he finds impressive: 452b–c, 452c–d, and 457b. (To these we might add 451b–c.) But even if Plato is referring to Aristophanes in these passages, he is probably *not* referring to the *Assembly of Women* directly, since they fall outside of Plato's discussion of the community of property, women, and children, and do not deal directly with anything found in the *Assembly of Women*. Thus, this second type of evidence is not strong either.

Adam calls the third type of evidence "the general resemblances between the two works in respect of subject-matter and content" (p. 350). He writes that in the more theoretical part of the *Assembly of Women*,

31

Aristophanes

> Aristophanes deals with a number of subjects which are treated also by Plato, viz. Community of Goods (590–594, 597–610, 673–692), Community of Women (611–634), Community of Children (635–650), the absence of every kind of [lawsuit] (657–672), and the establishment of [common meals] (715f.). The coincidence is remarkable and certainly requires explanation.[28]

This may be enough to make us doubt those who claim there is no connection between the two works, but if this is all there was, we would not be able to say anything else about what the connection actually is.

The final, and strongest, bits of evidence are the "specific parallels in idea, or in language, or in both idea and language" (pp. 350–52). Adam lists seven such parallels, and says, quite correctly in my view,

> These are more numerous and sometimes, perhaps, more remarkable than is generally supposed. . . . I am disposed to think that we should give preference to an explanation which, while it is probable on other grounds, leaves room for the possibility that some at least of these coincidences are not altogether fortuitous.[29]

Among those who have accepted a connection of some sort, what kinds of explanation have they offered? Adam lists three kinds, which pretty much exhaust the possibilities:

1. Aristophanes copies from Plato. Here the question of dating becomes essential. It is pretty much universally agreed that the *Assembly of Women* was performed in 392 (give or take a year). This means that in order for the *Republic* to have preceded it, Plato (b. 428?) would have to have written the

Republic when he was about thirty-five years old, which is highly improbable. But some respond that there may have been an earlier version, or that part (e.g., Books I–IV) may have been circulated earlier than the version that has come down to us. The issue of the unity of the *Republic* aside, Ussher (p. xvii) is right in saying, "Of course, there may have been an earlier edition, or part may have been issued in advance. But such hypotheses evince determination to establish a relationship at all costs."

2. Plato and Aristophanes are both borrowing from the same literary source. This position has been argued forcefully (but in the end, unconvincingly) by Ussher (pp. xviii–xx). It is, of course, possible; but there is in fact a better explanation.

3. Plato had the *Assembly of Women* in mind when he wrote the fifth book of the *Republic*. This position is, I think, the correct one. It is the position accepted by Adam (and, more recently, by Strauss and David, for example).[30] Adam writes that he is

> strongly inclined to admit the probability that Plato had the *Ecclesiazusae* and its author in his mind when he wrote that part of the fifth book which deals with the subject of women and children. Granted that the *Ecclesiazusae* is earlier than Book V of the *Republic*, Plato must have known the play, and the subjects treated of in the two writings are so closely allied that it would have been difficult to ignore the comedian altogether in traversing what is nearly the same ground. The positive coincidences, again, both general and particular, though they do not perhaps compel us to assume any connection between the two works, are, at all events in some cases, most readily explicable on that hypothesis.[31]

If Adam's view of the relationship between the two works is correct, then the *Assembly of Women* is indeed an extremely important work from the point of view of ancient Greek political thought.

5. TEXTUAL PROBLEMS

My translation is based on Ussher's edition of the text, which is generally held to be the best available. As with most Greek texts, the nature of the manuscripts of the *Assembly of Women* and the story of their transmission are complex, and scholarly disputes have arisen in numerous places over which reading to accept. I will not be getting into such things here, and I only rarely touch on them in the notes. I follow Ussher with few exceptions, none of which are terribly important.

There are, however, two textual problems worth mentioning here. Dover writes that Aristophanes left the reader

> to work out for himself how many characters there were in a play, which of them were present in a given scene, and who actually spoke a given line, [and] to construct from the text, as best he could, the movements, gestures and tones which in a modern dramatic text are prescribed in stage directions.[32]

So let me say a few words about stage directions and the identification of speakers.

Stage Directions

Lacking directions from the author, the editor or translator needs to include whatever directions are necessary for an intelligible reading of the play. This is what I have done. Fortunately, this is usually not so difficult or controversial—there are plenty of hints from the text itself. But I should briefly mention at this point one contentious issue concerning the staging of the play: the number of houses. There are generally held to be two houses onstage, though arguments have been presented both for one house and for three. Following a suggestion by Dover, I believe there should be three.[33] Of course, one's understanding and appreciation of the play will not depend on such an issue as this.

Identification of the Speakers

The manuscripts sometimes indicate who is speaking, but more often they simply indicate a change of speakers. As a result, much is left to interpretation, and some characters are quite problematic. For example, it is difficult to decide which lines should be given to the First Woman and which to the Second (30–282), and there are disputes over just how many lines should go to Chremes (372–477, 564–876). In fact, it is unclear precisely how many male characters there are in the play.[34] For the most part I follow Ussher, who, I believe, is quite sensible in these matters. But I do want to mention here one important case where I differ from Ussher and most others: the identification of the Master at the end of the play. The last scene begins with the appearance of a maid who has been sent by her mistress to fetch her master, the only person who has yet to attend the common dinner. The master soon arrives, and the scene centers around him. Who is he? Almost all scholars believe he is Blepyrus, and thus the maid is Praxagora's. But I believe S. Douglas Olson has successfully argued that the Master cannot be Blepyrus, and is in fact "an anonymous character, who appears onstage for the first time at 1128."[35] Against the view that the Master is Blepyrus, Olson writes:

> The identification of the Master with Blepyrus is actually open to decisive objections. At 725–27 Blepyrus declares that he is going off to the Agora to bask in his wife's reflected glory. This makes his return as the unfed [master] impossible. He can scarcely reappear later and be said to be going only now where we know he has already been and is in fact coming from, [the dinner] (1128, 1135) in the Agora. Nor does it make any sense that the Maid be unaware of his whereabouts (1125f.) when he is said to be precisely at her mistress's side (725). Ussher tries to dispose of these difficulties by manufacturing offstage activities for Blepyrus. Thus he conjectures that Blepyrus set off for the Agora with Praxagora but was "deflected . . . from his purpose on encountering the girls" [p. xxxiii]. Blepyrus, however, is not a real person with real offstage activities that can be reconstructed. He is a dramatic figment, a character who exists only onstage or in offstage activities specifically described onstage. Blepyrus says he is going to the Agora (725–27), so that is where he goes. . . . Blepyrus cannot be the [Master].[36]

Dover, who accepts the predominant view, writes:

On the assumptions that [the Master] is Blepyrus . . . , and
that the servant is Praxagora's, it's hard to see why he is late
for dinner, since Praxagora's husband said (725–727) that
he would stay close behind her; hard to see, that is, *if* we
respond to a joke by at once perceiving its incompatibility
with a different joke four hundred and sixty lines earlier.[37]

Well, of course, nearly anything is possible in Aristophanic comedy. It is true that in an issue like this, we are
dealing in probability and not certainty. Nevertheless, we
should accept what is most probable given the evidence,
which suggests Blepyrus is not the Master. Nor is it any of the
other male characters.[38] So the best candidate is a new, unnamed man. Olson writes:

The only realistic possibility is thus that the [Master] is an
anonymous character. Ussher (xxxiif.) maintains that this
a priori is unlikely. Like all such arguments, this one simply
assumes what it sets out to prove. In fact, there is a curious
air of anonymity throughout the final scenes of *Assembly of
Women*. Praxagora and Blepyrus, the central characters of
the first 700 lines of the play, disappear completely after
727. [Chremes and the Man] certainly do not approach
their stature. The Hags, the Young Girl, and . . . the Young
Man are all increasingly minor characters, many of whom
we have never seen before and will never see again. There
is no reason to be surprised when this turns out to be true
of the [Master] as well.[39]

In fact, given the nature of Praxagora's proposals, we should
not (after the "revolution") expect the play to focus on anyone
above average or with great ability—hence the mid-play disap-
pearance of Praxagora. Now this certainly does not rule out

Blepyrus, who is a buffoon and a mediocrity. But a more poignant ending is one which centers around a person who is no one in particular, an anybody. Such a person, after all, is the standard, the end, and the aim of Praxagora's egalitarianism.[40]

As an overview of the action of the play, I have included the Scenes of the play, and, in the case of the longest, Scene 1, the parts of the scene. These divisions are purely my invention, although I believe they follow naturally from the text.

Scene 1 (1–729): The women's revolution
    Praxagora's soliloquy (1–29)
    Rehearsal (30–168)
    Praxagora's speech (169–240)
    Last minute details (241–84)
    Parados (285–310)
    Blepyrus (311–477)
    Praxagora and the chorus (478–519)
    Praxagora and Blepyrus (520–70)
    Praxagora's communistic program (571–729)
Scene 2 (730–876): Chremes
Scene 3 (877–1111): The three hags
Scene 4 (1112–83): Off to the banquet

NOTES

1. On the chorus in the *Assembly of Women*, see Ussher, xxvii–xxxviii, and K. J. Dover, *Aristophanic Comedy* (Berkeley and Los Angeles: University of California Press, 1972), pp. 193–95.

2. In the last few years, the *Assembly of Women* has been receiving a lot of attention for its "political theory." See, for example,

Assembly of Women

E. David, *Aristophanes and Athenian Society of the Early Fourth Century* B.C. (Leiden: Brill, 1984), and A. W. Saxonhouse, *Fear of Diversity: The Birth of Political Science in Ancient Greek Thought* (Chicago: University of Chicago Press, 1992), Chapter 1, "A Tragicomic Prelude: Aristophanes' *Ecclesiazusae*."

3. Dover, *Aristophanic Comedy*, writes that "In Aristophanes' time, plays were performed at two great festivals in honour of the god Dionysos, the Lenaia (commonly corresponding to late January) and the City Dionysia (commonly late March) (p. 12). The number of comedies presented at each festival was three during the Peloponnesian War (431–404), and five before and after. Judges determined which play came in first, second, third, and so on. In some cases we know where a play was performed and how well it did. For example, the *Acharnians* took first prize at the Lenaia (in 422). But we do not know how well the *Assembly of Women* did, or where it was performed.

4. On date of the play, see Ussher, xviii–xx, and Dover, *Aristophanic Comedy*, 190.

5. An obol equals one-sixth of a drachma (in other words, it's not much money). See David, *Aristophanes and Athenian Society*, and K. S. Rothwell, *Politics and Persuasion in Aristophanes'* Ecclesiazusae (Leiden: Brill, 1990).

6. Some would disagree with this: For example, Rothwell, *Politics and Persuasion*, believes that although Aristophanes is not a supporter of the views of Praxagora, the *Assembly of Women* is nonetheless not "an earnest attack on communism" (p. 9). Rather, he believes Aristophanes uses the utopian communism of the *Assembly of Women* as a means of attacking the "selfishness" of the people. I believe that whatever else it impugns, this play is also a serious attack on communism. This will hopefully be made clear in what follows. But for now, note that more space is devoted to the presentation of Praxagora's communistic program, and to the follies of that program, than to any other issue in the play.

7. Cf. *Politics* II.5.1263a8–15, where Aristotle is criticizing the communism of property of Plato's *Republic* (N.B.: Unless otherwise noted, translations from the Greek are my own):

Aristophanes

Now if the farmers were others than the citizens, the manner in which property would be managed would be different and easier; but if the citizens do the hard work themselves, the matters connected with possessions will lead to greater discontent. For in fact, when in the enjoyment of things and in work they are not equal, but unequal, accusations will necessarily be raised against those enjoying or taking many things while laboring little, by those taking less while laboring more.

8. Felix Jacoby, *Fragmente der griechischen Historiker* (Berlin: Weidmann, 1927–1957; Leiden: Brill, 1958–), fr. 31.

9. W. W. How and J. Wells, *A Commentary on Herodotus* (Oxford: Oxford University Press, 1912), 1:339.

10. The *Assembly of Women* was produced about ten years after the defeat of Athens by Sparta in the Peloponnesian War. Following its defeat, Athens's economy worsened (though perhaps not as badly as is sometimes suggested), and there existed (as before the war) tensions between rich and poor, and between moderate democrats, radical democrats, and those with a more oligarchic slant. In general, however well Athens was able to recover from its defeat, it was not in the same shape it had been before the outbreak of hostilities.

11. There are modern parallels: Reports from the South Pacific in the eighteenth century (picked up by Rousseau, for instance), and the views of twentieth-century Marxist anthropologists on primitive societies. For a good example of a romanticized (and inaccurate) picture of tribal life, see Herman Melville's *Typee* (1846), especially chapter 17. N. McInnes, in "Communism" (*Encyclopedia of Philosophy*, 1972 ed.), writes:

Sound information played no role in the many communist projects. Their authors were content with tenuous legends (the Atlantis of Plato's *Critias* or the Sparta of Plutarch's *Lycurgus*) or with scraps of misinformation ("noble savages" in the New World).

(Not every report the Greeks received was positive, e.g., Xenophon, *Anabasis* V.4.33–34, Apollonius Rhodius III.1023–25).

12. See Plutarch, *Lycurgus* I, and Herodotus I.65.

13. See A. H. M Jones, *Sparta* (Oxford: Blackwell, 1967), p. 4.

14. See R. Talbert, *Plutarch on Sparta* (Harmondsworth, England: Penguin Books, 1988), pp. 164–66.

15. But see *Republic* 599d, and *Laws* 625c–e, 636a–b, 762c, 780a–c, 780e–781a.

16. See Xenophon, *Lakedaimonian Constitution* VII.1–3; Plutarch, *Lycurgus* IX.1, XIII.5, XXV.3; Aristotle, *Politics* 1270a15–29.

17. On the equality of possession, see Plutarch, *Lycurgus* IX.1–3.

18. See Polybius VI.45, 48. Aristotle says the land ended up in the hands of a few (*Politics* 1270a15–29, 1307a36). Jones, *Sparta*, p. 43, calls the Lycurgan distribution of land a fourth-century myth (cf. Talbert, *Plutarch on Sparta*, pp. 185–86).

19. See Xenophon, *Lakedaimonian Constitution* VI.3–5, and Aristotle, *Politics* 1263a35ff. Aristotle does not regard this as an instance of the communism of property.

20. See Xenophon, *Lakedaimonian Constitution* I.5–9, and Plutarch, *Lycurgus* XV.10–13.

21. See Xenophon, *Lakedaimonian Constitution* I.5–9, and Plutarch, *Lycurgus* XV.15–18.

22. F. W. Walbank, *A Historical Commentary on Polybius*, 3 vols. (Oxford: Oxford University Press, 1967), 1:340–41.

23. See Plutarch, *Lycurgus* XV.7–14, XVI.1, XVII.1.

24. Jones, *Sparta*, p. 34.

25. See Plutarch, *Lycurgus* XXIV.1, XXV.5.

26. A. Nauck, *Tragicorum Craecorum Fragmenta*, 2d ed., supplemented by B. Snell (Hildesheim, 1964).

27. J. Adam, ed., *The Republic of Plato*, 2 vols. (Cambridge: Cambridge University Press, 1902), 1:345–55.

28. Ibid., p. 350.

29. Ibid., pp. 350–52.

30. L. Strauss, *Aristophanes and Socrates* (New York, Basic Books, 1966), and David, *Aristophanes and Athenian Society*.

31. Adam, *The Republic of Plato*, p. 354.
32. Dover, *Aristophanic Comedy*, p. 10.
33. Ibid., pp. 197–98.
34. Ibid., pp. 195–96.
35. S. D. Olson, "The Identity of the Δεσπότης at *Ecclesiazusae* 1128f," *Greek, Roman and Byzantine Studies* 28 (1987): 161–66.
36. Ibid., p. 162.
37. Dover, *Aristophanic Comedy*, p. 193 n. 3.
38. Olson also shows that the Master cannot be Chremes or the Youth (pp. 163, 165). He argues less successfully for ruling out the man who argues with Chremes over turning in one's goods. A case could in fact be made for this man, though it is not without its problems (see Olson, "The Identity of the Δεσπότης," pp. 163–165) and thus is not as strong as the case for a new, anonymous character.
39. Olson, "The Identity of the Δεσπότης," p. 165.
40. Cf. ibid., p. 166.

Assembly of Women

SCENE ONE

A street in Athens. There are three houses[1] set close together, each with a front door and an upstairs window. In this scene the center house belongs to Blepyrus and Praxagora. The house on the right is Chremes', and the house on the left belongs to the Man and his wife, the Second Woman. It is still dark, but dawn is about an hour away. Praxagora comes out of her house wearing her husband's clothes and carrying a fake beard, her husband's walking stick, some wreaths, and a lamp. She moves to the left of the house on the left, sets the lamp on a pedestal of some kind, and looks around. She then begins to address the lamp in an almost hymnal tone, as if it were a god.[2]

PRAXAGORA: *O radiant light from crafted lamp, finest of those invented by the most skillful potters. We shall reveal your birth and fortune: By the wheel set in motion, born from the force of the* 5 *potter, you, with your nostrils,[3] hold the radiant office of the sun. Launch the agreed-upon symbol of flame!* [She pulls the wick to make the light burn brighter.] *We reveal this to you alone, for even while we are in our bedrooms, engaged in Aphrodesian acro-* 10 *batics, you stand close by, overseer of our writhing bodies, and no one bars your eye from the room. And you alone shine into the*

---

1. See Dover, *Aristophanic Comedy* (Berkeley and Los Angeles: University of California Press, 1972), p. 198.

2. This speech is "a comic eulogy of common objects like a lamp." Praxagora's address to the lamp is like an address "to the Sun-god" (U, 70).

3. "As applied to a lamp, [nostril] is the round hole on the snout (so to call it) of the lamp, through which the lighted wick protrudes . . ." (R, 4).

secret nooks between our thighs, while you singe off the surfacing
15 *hair.*[4] *And as we secretly open the storehouses full of grain and the*
stream of Bacchus, you stand by to assist. And when you help us
in doing these things, you do not babble to our neighbors. Because
of all of this you will also share in our present plans which, at the
Scira,[5] *my friends resolved to carry out.* [She begins to speak
normally.] But not one of those who was supposed to be here
20 is present. And yet it's nearly dawn, at which time the
Assembly will begin forthwith. But to claim our seats, we
"courtesans" (as Phyromachus once said, if you still remember) must go unnoticed when we sit down.[6] So what
25 could be the matter? Perhaps they weren't able to stitch on
the beards they were told to have with them? Or perhaps it
was difficult for them to steal their husband's cloaks without
getting caught? But I see some lamp coming this way. I'll
retreat in case it's actually some *man* approaching.

**Praxagora withdraws beside the house, leaving the lamp. A
few women arrive, each dressed as a man and carrying a man's
walking stick and a fake beard. (The Chorus of Women**

---

4. Depilation, through singeing off with a lamp or plucking, was a
common practice in Greece.

5. "The parasol festival; a festival celebrated by the women alone,
at midsummer, in the month Scirophorion, in honour of Athene Sciras."
(R, 6).

6. It is unclear who Phyromachus is and why he is mentioned here.
(There are also some problems with the text. Ussher transposes lines 22
and 23, but I translate them in their manuscript order.) Phyromachus may
have been a tragic actor known for slips of the tongue or incorrect pro-
nunciation. Perhaps he once said "courtesans" (ἑταίρας) when he meant
to say "seats" (ἕδρας).

assemble silently, a few at a time, between lines 30 and 56. Each member of the Chorus is dressed as a man and is carrying a walking stick and fake beard.[7])

FIRST WOMAN: Time to go. For just now as we were ap- 30 proaching, the herald, for the second time, crowed.[8]

PRAXAGORA [in front of the house on the left]: I've been waiting here watching for you *all* night. But now I'll call my neighbor here, gently tapping on her door (for her husband mustn't notice). [She taps on her neighbor's door.] 35

Second Woman [the neighbor]: Yes, yes, I heard the scratching of your fingers while I was slipping into my shoes, for I wasn't sleeping. You see, dear, the man I'm married to is Salaminian: He rowed me the whole night in the sheets, such that I just now grabbed his cloak.[9] 40

PRAXAGORA: Oh, I see Cleinarete and Sostrata are here, and Philainete.

FIRST WOMAN: Shouldn't you be hurrying? For Glyce swore that the one who came last would have to pay us nine quarts 45 of wine and one quart of chickpeas.

---

7. On the chorus in the *Assembly of Women*, see Dover, *Aristophanic Comedy*, p. 193.

8. This is most likely an instance of a contrary-to-expectation (παρὰ προσδοκίαν) joke. The audience expects a word that describes something a herald does, only to find out the "herald" is a rooster. (This also indicates the time of day: it is still dark, but dawn is approaching.)

9. Salaminians were very often oarsmen.

47

SECOND WOMAN: And don't you see Melistiche, the wife of Smicythion, hurrying into her shoes?

FIRST WOMAN: Yes, it seems to me that she alone was able to get away from her husband at leisure.

SECOND WOMAN: And don't you see Geusistrate the tavern
50 keeper's wife holding the torch in her right hand?

FIRST WOMAN: And I see the wives of Philodoterus and Chairetades approaching, and very many other women who are a credit to the city.

CHORUS LEADER: Yes, and I for my part got away and sneaked
55 here with a great deal of hardship, my dear. For my husband was coughing the whole night, having stuffed himself full of anchovies in the evening.[10]

PRAXAGORA [seeing that they have assembled]: Settle down! Since you're all here, let me begin. I need to ask you whether you have done what at the Scira we resolved to do.

FIRST WOMAN: I have. First, I have armpits thicker than a
60 bush, just like we agreed. And when my husband went to the marketplace, I oiled my whole body and tanned myself, standing in the sun the whole day.

---

10. "[T]heir fine *hair*-bones . . . would cause the husband's trouble" (U, 82, original italics).

SECOND WOMAN: Me, too. But first I threw my razor out of the house, so that I would grow hairy all over and no longer 65 resemble a woman.

PRAXAGORA: But do you have the beards which you all were told to have for this meeting?

FIRST WOMAN [displaying hers]: By Hecate, I have this fine 70 one.

SECOND WOMAN [displaying hers]: And I have one much finer than Epicrates'.[11]

PRAXAGORA [pointing to the Chorus of Women]: And what do they say?

FIRST WOMAN [seeing the Chorus nodding yes]: They say they do—they are nodding yes at any rate.

PRAXAGORA: And I see that you have done all the rest, for you have Laconian shoes,[12] walking sticks, and men's cloaks, 75 as we agreed.

FIRST WOMAN: I was at least able secretly to carry off Lamias' staff as he lay sleeping.

---

11. A politician famous for his facial hairiness.
12. A type of men's shoe.

SECOND WOMAN: Oh yes, this is the staff of the one who farts.[13]

80 **PRAXAGORA:** By Zeus the Savior, he is well suited for being clad in the hide worn by the all-seeing, if indeed someone else is to tend the public executioner.[14] But come now, we must do what remains to be done while the stars are still in the sky. For 85 the Assembly, which we have prepared to enter, will commence at dawn.

---

13. "His name [Lamias] affords a handle for the unseemly jest . . . which is based on an incident in the old legends about the ogress Lamia" (R, 15). Rogers notes that according to the scholiast, the comic Crates wrote of Lamia: "having a staff, she farted." In the *Wasps* Aristophanes mentions the story of how "Lamia farted when they caught her" (1177). Beyond this, I do not know the point of the joke, and perhaps there was none: "Undoubtedly the breaking of wind could be counted on to raise a laugh when all else failed" (H, 422).

14. The references to Lamias, to the all-seeing, and to the public executioner, are very difficult to interpret (and their meaning may well be lost to us). The following remarks (which represent just one interpretation) are for the most part based on the short article by Ian Worthington, "Aristophanes Ecclesiazusae 76–81 and Argus," *American Journal of Philology* 108 (1987): 161–64: The all-seeing refers to Argus, the hundred-eyed guardian of Io. The joke is aimed at Lamias, who was possibly poor, and a jailer in charge of those prisoners waiting execution. (In this sense he "looked after" the public executioner.) Possessing a large staff or club, and wearing the hide of the hundred-eyed, all-seeing Argus—he was perhaps wearing a very tattered shirt, since he could not afford a new one—would have helped Lamias in watching the prisoners. ("[I]n comedy often the dress of a specific individual invests the wearer with that individual's characteristics," p. 162). (And yet his wife is able to escape.) See also U, 86.

FIRST WOMAN: Yes, by Zeus, we must, so that you can grab us seats below the speakers' platform, facing the prytanes.[15]

SECOND WOMAN [carrying some wool and brushes for carding wool]: By Zeus, I brought these, you know, so that I could do some carding while the Assembly fills up.

PRAXAGORA: "Fills up," you wretch?   90

SECOND WOMAN: By Artemis, I have. Can't I listen while carding? Besides, my children are naked.

PRAXAGORA: "Carding" indeed! You, who mustn't uncover any part of your body while sitting there! It would be a fine 95 thing indeed if the Assembly was full, and then one of us, stepping over someone already seated, threw back her cloak and revealed her Phormisius.[16] But if we sit still in the front with our cloaks wrapped around us, we will go unnoticed. And with the beards we'll have on when we sit there, who seeing 100 us will not believe we are men? In this way Agyrrhius, who had the beard of Pronomus, went unnoticed, even though ear-

---

15. The "presidents" who presided over each Assembly.

16. Another contrary-to-expectation joke. Phormisius was famous for his hairiness.

Praxagora seems to be making two related complaints: (1) If the Second Woman cards her wool while the Assembly fills, she would have to sit in a revealing way with one leg raised and her clothes tucked up (not to mention the feminine nature of the activity); (2) if she cards her wool while the Assembly is filling up, which makes her late, and she then tries to get a seat when it is nearly full, she may have to step over someone and thereby give away the conspiracy.

lier he was a woman. But now, as you can see, he manages the
105 greatest affairs in the city.[17] Indeed, by the coming day,[18] it's
because of him that we undertake this daring deed, if in some
way we are able to take over the affairs of the city and do the
city some good. For now we neither run nor row.[19]

FIRST WOMAN: But how can a gathering of female-minded
110 women address the Assembly?

PRAXAGORA: Actually, rather well, I think. For they say that
the young who are banged the most are the most skillful
speakers. And as luck will have it, this is an attribute of ours.

115 FIRST WOMAN: I don't know. Lack of experience is terrible.

PRAXAGORA: Is this not the reason we have gathered here, so
that we could rehearse what we must say there? [Impatiently
addressing the First Woman] You can't be fast enough strap-
ping on your beard, and the same goes for you others who
have practiced speaking.

120 FIRST WOMAN: One of us didn't know how to speak, dear?

---

17. "Agyrrhius's career was going nowhere until he became a pathic:
now he is an important official. . . ." (H, 458) Pronomus was probably his lover.

18. This was perhaps a common oath of Athenian women (R, 20),
particularly relevant given their upcoming day.

19. This can be taken in one of two ways: (1) the city isn't going
anywhere, or (2) as it is, women cannot do anything in the city. See U, 90.

PRAXAGORA: Come, then, put that beard on and quickly become a man. And I will set down the garlands[20] and put mine on, the same as you, since it might seem to me a good idea to say something.

Praxagora and a few others put on their beards.

SECOND WOMAN: Look here, O sweetest Praxagora, dear girl. 125
This seems so ridiculous.

PRAXAGORA: How is it ridiculous?

SECOND WOMAN: It's as if some cuttlefish, having been fried, put on a beard.[21]

PRAXAGORA [ignoring the Second Woman's remark, and speaking in an official manner, in the role of herald]: O *Purifier, carry round the polecat.*[22] *Come forward.* [As if addressing someone in the audience] Ariphrades, stop talking.[23] [She resumes her offi- 130 cial tone.] *Come and sit. Who wishes to address the Assembly?*

---

20. I.e., the wreaths for the speakers.

21. Perhaps the tanned women are thought to resemble fried cuttle-fish in color.

22. Another contrary-to-expectation joke. The Purifier "was the officer who purified the place of the Assembly. . . . But the animal he carried was a young *pig* . . . , not a *cat*. . . . Doubtless the polecat, as a *house* pet . . . would come to mind more readily for women" (U, 93).

23. Aristophanes elsewhere claims that someone named Ariphrades invented cunnilingus (see *Wasps* 1280ff. and *Knights* 1281ff.). So Aristophanes is here either making fun of this same person (he can't keep his mouth shut, even while attending a play) (see H, 389), or perhaps Aristophanes is referring to another, garrulous Ariphrades (U, 93).

FIRST WOMAN: I do.

PRAXAGORA: *Then put on the garland, and good fortune be with you.*

FIRST WOMAN [puts on the garland and steps forward]: There. [She pauses, as if waiting for her cue.]

PRAXAGORA: Please speak.

FIRST WOMAN: Shouldn't I drink before I speak?

PRAXAGORA: Drink, indeed!

FIRST WOMAN: Then why was this garland put on me, dear?

135 PRAXAGORA: Get away from here. Is this what you'd have done there, too?

FIRST WOMAN: What? Don't they drink in the Assembly?

PRAXAGORA: There you go again—"drink."

FIRST WOMAN: Yes, by Artemis, and their wine is unmixed, too. For if you reflect on their deliberations, why, it's just as if
140 they were dead drunk. And further, by Zeus, they pour libations; or why would they say such prayers, if wine were not present? And they quarrel like men who have had too much to drink, and the archers carry out the one who acts up because of wine.

PRAXAGORA: You, go and sit; you're worthless.

FIRST WOMAN [taking her seat]: By Zeus, it really would've 145
been better for me without a beard. For I'm dying of thirst, I am.

PRAXAGORA: Does someone else wish to speak?

SECOND WOMAN: I do.

PRAXAGORA: Come then, put on this garland—for in fact our
business is underway. Now speak like a man, and well, leaning 150
in the proper fashion upon your cane.

**SECOND WOMAN [puts on a garland and steps forward and
speaks as if she were a man addressing the Assembly]:** *I should
have liked one of those accustomed to speaking to say what is best,
in which case I would have sat quietly. But as it is, I for one will
not allow them to put tanks in the taverns—for water.*[24] *This does
not seem good to me, by the two gods.*[25] 155

PRAXAGORA [snatching the garland from her]: "By the two
gods?" Girl, have you lost your mind?

SECOND WOMAN: What's wrong? I certainly didn't ask you for
a drink.

---

24. Perhaps this is a contrary-to-expectation joke: she is against the
existence of tanks in taverns *for water* (but not for wine, of course).

25. A favorite oath of Athenian *women*. The two gods are Demeter
and Persephone.

55

PRAXAGORA: No, by Zeus, but you're a man and you swore by the two gods. The other things, though, were said most astutely.

SECOND WOMAN: O yes, by Apollo!

160 **PRAXAGORA:** Stop, then, because I won't advance another step toward taking part in the Assembly unless this is perfected.

SECOND WOMAN: Give me back the garland, and I'll speak
165 again. For I think I've got the right idea now. *O Assembled Women. . . .*

PRAXAGORA: Wretch, are you calling men women again?

SECOND WOMAN [pointing to someone in the audience]: It was because of that Epigonus. I looked in his direction and thought that I was speaking to women.

170 **PRAXAGORA [taking the garland]:** You, go and sit down over there as well. **[The Second Woman does so.]** For your sake I think it is best for me to take this garland and speak myself. I pray to the gods that we succeed in accomplishing the things we have resolved to do. **[She begins her speech.]** *The concerns*
175 *of this our land are the same for me as they are for you; and I grieve and endure the gravity of all the affairs of the city. For I see the city forever using statesmen who are worthless. And if someone is*
180 *worthy for a single day, he is worthless for ten. You turn it over to another, he'll do much worse. Now it's difficult to advise peevish men: you fear those who want to love you, and always supplicate those who do not. Once it was the case that we almost never made*
185 *use of the Assembly, but we did think Agyrrhius was worthless.*

Now we use it regularly, and the one who gets money praises him to the skies, while the one who does not says that those seeking to be paid in the Assembly are worthy of death.[26]

FIRST WOMAN: By Aphrodite, you said that well!

PRAXAGORA: You swore by Aphrodite, dear? It would be just 190 beautiful if you were to say that in the Assembly!

FIRST WOMAN: But I wouldn't say it there.

PRAXAGORA: Then don't make a habit of saying it now. [She continues her speech.] *When we considered this League[27] again, it seemed that unless it came into being, the city would be destroyed. But* 195 *when it finally came into being, the people were annoyed, and the speaker who persuaded them of this at once ran away and left. It is necessary to launch ships: It seems good to the poor man, but not to the rich or to the farmers. You were annoyed with the Corinthians, and they with you; now they are useful, you make yourselves useful too.* 200 *The Argives are fools, but Hieronymus is wise. Safety peeped her head out, but Thrasybulus himself is angry at not being summoned to help.*[28]

26. "Praxagora is contrasting the state of things *before*, with the state of things *after*, the introduction by Agyrrhius of the [three-obol wage for going to the Assembly]" (R, 30). Agyrrhius was responsible for the initial (one obol) fee for attending the Assembly, and for later raising it from two to three obols.

27. The anti-Spartan League of 395 B.C.E.

28. "The Argives [who were among the allies of Athens against Sparta] had been vehement opponents of a peace which Hieronymus (it seems) supported. 'Yet when peace . . . *does* pop its head out, you again demonstrate your indecisiveness by failing to call on Thrasybulus' (Praxagora's *own* recipe for 'salvation')" (U, xxiv).

FIRST WOMAN: What an intelligent man!

PRAXAGORA: Now you praise me well. [She continues.] *You,*
205 *people, are the cause of this. For receiving your wages from the public*
funds, each one of you individually seeks to gain something, but the
210 *community roams about like Aisimus.*[29] *However, if you do what I*
propose, you may still be saved. I say that we must hand over the city
to the women! For in fact, we use them in our households as admin-
istrators and treasurers.

All applaud.

FIRST WOMAN: Bravo, bravo, by Zeus, bravo!

SECOND WOMAN: Speak on, speak on, good man!

PRAXAGORA [continuing]: *That they are better in their ways than*
215 *we are I shall demonstrate. First, they dye their wool with hot water,*
according to ancient custom—every single one of them, and you won't
see them making radical changes.[30] *(But if things were going well, the*
city of Athens would not be in favor of being saved unless some novel
things were wastefully worked for.)
220   *They do the cooking sitting down, as of old.*
They carry things on their heads, as of old.

---

29. The scholiast says Aisimus was lame and stupid.

30. "Making radical changes" is how I translate μεταπειρωμένας.
"The word is (ironically) ἅπαξ λεγόμενον [the only instance of the word
we know of]" (U, 105). It is ironic in two ways: (1) It may very well be a
neologism—itself something radically new. (2) This radically new word
referring to radical change is used to describe women who are supposed to
be conservative (but, we shall see, have very revolutionary intentions).

They hold their Thesmophoria,[31] *as of old.*
They bake their flat cakes,[32] *as of old.*
They distress their husbands, as of old.
They have their lovers indoors, as of old.   225
They buy themselves things on the side, as of old.
They love their wine unmixed, as of old.
They enjoy being fucked,[33] *as of old.*
   So, gentlemen, let us turn over the city to them, and not babble   230
nor inquire about what they intend to do, but simply allow them to
rule, considering this alone: That being mothers of soldiers first,
they will desire to save them. Next, provisions: Who would send a   235
soldier more than the one who bore him? A woman is best at raising
money, and when in power she would never be cheated, for women
themselves are used to cheating. But I'll pass over the other
points.[34] *If you are persuaded by me on this, you will go through life*   240
being happy.

FIRST WOMAN: Good, sweetest Praxagora, and shrewd.
Where, my dear, did you learn to speak so beautifully?

---

31. Aristophanes devotes a whole play (*Thesmophoriazusae*) to this
women's festival.

32. Baking flat cakes (sticking them in the oven) may refer to sexual
intercourse (H, 177).

33. Rogers translates this as "They like a woman's pleasures," but the
Greek is βινούμεναι χαίνουσιν, which is much coarser. Henderson
writes: "The vulgar *vox propria* for sexual intercourse in comedy is βινεῖν,
which seems to have had the same force and flexibility in Greek as *fuck*
does in English. The connotation is always of violent and/or illicit intercourse. [The sexual meaning of] κινεῖν . . . came to be identical in usage to
the straightforwardly obscene βινεῖν . . ." (205).

34. Namely, her entire communistic program.

PRAXAGORA: I lived with my husband in the Pnyx among the refugees.[35] When I heard the speakers I learned from them.

245 FIRST WOMAN: Then it's not for nothing, dear, that you're clever and wise. We women will choose you as leader on the spot if you achieve what you intend. But suppose Cephalus[36] abuses you, perish the thought, how will you reply to him in the Assembly?

250 PRAXAGORA: I'll say he's out of his mind.

FIRST WOMAN: But everyone knows that already.

PRAXAGORA: But I'll say he's deranged.

FIRST WOMAN: They know that, too.

PRAXAGORA: But I'll also say he molds his pottery badly, but the city well and beautifully.[37]

SECOND WOMAN: But what if Neocleides the bleary-eyed abuses you?

35. The Pnyx is the hill where the Assembly took place. "The refugees" is probably a reference to "the flight of the Athenians from the islands and seaports into the city before the conquering progress of Lysander," who compelled the Athenians he found to return to Athens. "It is to this immigration at the close, and not to that at the beginning, of the Peloponnesian War that Praxagora's statement refers" (R, 41).
36. A famous orator and radical democrat. As we shall see, he was probably also known as a pretty poor potter.
37. I.e., he is a better politician than he is a potter, and we all know how bad a politician he is.

PRAXAGORA: I'll say that he looks up a dog's ass.[38]   255

SECOND WOMAN: But what if they strike you down?

PRAXAGORA: I'll move forward, not being unaccustomed to many strokes.[39]

FIRST WOMAN: There's only one thing left to consider: what if the archers drag you off, what will you do?

PRAXAGORA: I'll stick out my elbows like this [she demon-   260
strates], for I'll never be seized in the middle.[40]

CHORUS LEADER: And if they lift you, we'll order them to let you go.

FIRST WOMAN: We've prepared these things beautifully, but we haven't thought about this: how we'll remember to raise our hands there. For we're used to raising our legs.   265

---

38. The scholiast says this was a proverb spoken to the short-sighted, and that Neocleides was, among other things, an orator and a sycophant. Perhaps Praxagora's reply is meant as an abusive remedy for blindness.

39. The word ὑποκρούειν can mean both "strike down" and "interrupt." "Interrupt" better captures what the Second Woman is asking, but I want to make clear the connection between "strike down" in her line, and the related word (with sexual connotations) "κρουμάτων" ("strokes") in Praxagora's response.

40. This might be a play on words lost in translation, for in Greek to grab someone in the middle can refer both to a move in wrestling and to grabbing a person's genitals. (See H, 236.)

Aristophanes

PRAXAGORA: That's a difficult thing. But all the same, we must raise one arm, bare to the shoulder. Come now, tuck up
270 your tunic. Quickly slip into those Laconian shoes, as you have often seen your husbands do when they are about to walk to the Assembly, or any time they go outdoors. Next, when you have done all of this well, strap on your beards. And when you've got them on correctly, fitting all around, you can
275 also throw on your husbands' cloaks, which you stole; and then, leaning on your walking sticks, go, singing some old man's song, mimicking the ways of country folk.

280 **FIRST WOMAN:** You speak well. But let us go on ahead of them, for I know that other women too will come from the country straight to the Pnyx.

PRAXAGORA: But hurry, as it is the custom there that those who are not present at the Pnyx by dawn must slip away without even a clothespin.[41]

Praxagora and the First and Second Women exit. The Chorus remains.[42]

---

41. This is perhaps a double entendre—one that is especially comic coming from women pretending to be men.

42. "After the actors' departure the Chorus complete their preparations. They split into two groups [the strophe and antistrophe], the first one more concerned with establishing their new male role securely . . . , the second group more specifically acting . . . as dwellers in the country. . . . This is technically the πάροδος: the point at which the Chorus file into the orchestra along the passageways (πάροδοι). But in this play . . . a formal πάροδος is dispensed with, and the following choric passages are sung as the women *leave*, not *enter*, the orchestra" (U, 114).

62

CHORUS LEADER: It is time for us to proceed, *Gentlemen.* You 285
must always say this word, having memorized it, lest it elude
you. For the risk is not small if we are caught putting on so
great a daring deed in the dark.

STROPHE:

To the Assembly, *Gentlemen,*   290
For the magistrate has warned
That he who isn't there on time,
By the very early morn—
Dusty from great hurrying, and
Sour from the time of day,
Garlic smellin' from a hurried meal—
Will forfeit his three-obol pay.

Now you, Charitimides,
And Draces and Smicythes,
Follow us, don't lag behind.
Come on now, pick up the pace.   295
Oh, and when you put on this show,
Take care lest you strike a wrong note.
We'll all grab our seats together, .
And together as sisters we'll vote.
(What are we saying? We must call them *brothers!*[43])

ANTISTROPHE:

See to it that we push aside   300
All the incoming city men,

---

43. Observe that they immediately strike the wrong note.

Who when the pay was an obol,
Stayed in the market babblin'.
But now that the pay has improved—
It's no longer a mere tuppence—
They flock to the Assembly,
Yes, they've become quite a nuisance.

When noble Myronides ruled
305 Men would assemble without pay,
Each carrying wine and olives
And bread and onions for the day.
Now for each public service done,
They look to get three obols pay,
310 Just like common laborers
Carrying mortar and clay.

**The entire Chorus exits. A few moments later, Blepyrus (Prax-
agora's husband) comes out of his (the center) house, dressed in
his wife's saffron nightgown and Persian slippers. He is in obvious
discomfort. (It is now a bit lighter out than it was before.)**

BLEPYRUS: What's the matter? Where's my wife gone? It's
nearly dawn, and she's nowhere to be seen. I've just been lying
in bed needing to relieve myself, looking to grab my shoes and
315 cloak in the dark. But when, after groping about, I was unable
to find them, and the dung man kept banging at my back
door, I grabbed my wife's nightgown, and slipped into her Per-
320 sian shoes. But where, where can a person relieve oneself in
the clear? Or perhaps at night anywhere is fine? No one will
see me relieving myself now. Woe is me. It's ill fortune that I
took a wife in old age. For that I deserve to be beaten. For she's

gone out intending to do no good. But all the same I *must* find   325
a spot to relieve myself.

Blepyrus's neighbor comes out of his house (on the left). He, too, is dressed in *his* wife's nightgown and slippers.

MAN: Who is this? Not my neighbor Blepyrus?

BLEPYRUS: By Zeus, it's the man himself.

MAN: Tell me, what's that brown on you? Surely Cinesias   330
didn't crap on you from somewhere?[44]

BLEPYRUS: No, but I had to go out, so I put on my wife's little saffron dress.

MAN: But where is your cloak?

BLEPYRUS: I couldn't say. I searched, but didn't find it among the bedclothes.

MAN: Then why didn't you tell your wife to show you?   335

BLEPYRUS: Because, by Zeus, she doesn't happen to be home. She slipped out of the house without my noticing, and I fear she's doing something revolutionary.

MAN: By Poseidon, then, you have experienced the very same things I have. For my wife, too, is gone, having taken my   340

---

44. He was infamous for having befouled a shrine to Hecate.

cloak with her. And this doesn't bother me much, but she took my shoes as well. At least I wasn't able to find them anywhere.

345 BLEPYRUS: By Dionysus, I couldn't find my Laconians, but as I had to relieve myself, I slipped my feet into her shoes and went out so that I wouldn't soil the blanket, for it was clean. But what could be the matter? Is it not that your wife was asked to breakfast by one of her friends?

350 MAN: I guess so. At least she's not bad, as far as I know. But you're letting down some kind of rope. As for me, it's time to go to the Assembly, after I get my cloak, which is the only one I have.

355 BLEPYRUS: Me, too, once I've finished letting it down. But now some pear keeps blocking my food.

MAN: Isn't that what Thrasybulus said to the Spartans?[45]

The Man exits.

BLEPYRUS: By Dionysus, it's seized me tightly. But what am I
360 going to do? And this is not my only grief. It remains to be seen where my dung will go when I eat. For now this man from Pearville, whoever he is, has bolted the door.[46] So who

---

45. It is unclear to what precisely this refers, but it must have something to do with a military blockade—perhaps of food supplies—of or by the Spartans.

46. Pearville (Ἀχραδούσιας) is very likely a play on the name of an actual deme (or region of Attica), Ἀχερδούσιος.

will fetch a doctor for me, and what kind of doctor? Which of
the anal experts is skilled in the art I require? Does Amynon   365
know? But perhaps he will refuse.[47] Someone call Antisthenes,
at all costs. For this man (judging from his groans) knows
what an anus relieving itself needs.[48] [Speaking in a tragic
tone] *O Queen Eileithyia, do not overlook me—bursting yet*   370
bolted shut—lest I become a dung-filled comic commode.[49]

It is now past dawn. Chremes walks onstage and is headed in
the direction of his house (on the right). He stops when he
sees Blepyrus.

CHREMES: Hello there, what are you doing? Surely you're not
relieving yourself?

BLEPYRUS: Me? Definitely not yet, by Zeus, rather I'm getting
up. [He stands up.]

CHREMES: But you're wearing your wife's tunic!

BLEPYRUS: Yes, for inside in the dark I happened to grab it.   375
But tell me, where are *you* coming from?

CHREMES: From the Assembly.

---

47. This is one of the readings Ussher suggests. It is ironical:
"Amynon has never refused any similar assignment" (U, 127).

48. Amynon and Antisthenes are no doubt pathics (see H, 472). Antisthenes may also suffer from chronic constipation. (See lines 806–808 below.)

49. This is a parody of a prayer offered by women in labor. Eileithya
is the patron goddess of childbirth.

BLEPYRUS: Has it been dismissed already?

CHREMES: By Zeus, very early. And in fact, dear Zeus, the red paint that they sprinkled around caused a great deal of laughter.[50]

380 BLEPYRUS: But did you get your three obols?

CHREMES: I wish I had. But I got there too late and am thus ashamed, by Zeus, that I have nothing but my empty wallet.

BLEPYRUS: But what was the cause of this?

CHREMES: A very large group of people, such as there's never
385 been, came en masse to the Pnyx. And when we saw them we thought they all looked like shoemakers. It really was extraordinary to see such pale faces in the Assembly. As a result, though, I myself and many others didn't get anything.

BLEPYRUS: Would I get anything if I went right now?

390 CHREMES: Are you kidding? By Zeus, not if you had gone when the cock was crowing for the second time.

50. "[B]efore payment was introduced for attendance at meetings of the Assembly . . . , the citizens had sometimes to be rounded up (by the Scythian archers . . .) and forced to carry out their public duty. This was done by a rope smeared with vermilion. . . . Those who got smeared with the vermilion were fined. . . . But here there is no question of reluctance: on the contrary, the meeting is over . . . before it was scheduled to begin. It is thus best . . . to suppose that the archers use the paint to exclude those who (though coming early . . .) arrive to discover the 'house' full. But it must be doubted whether such a situation would ever (outside comedy) arise" (U, 129).

BLEPYRUS [in a tragic tone]: *Oh wretched me! Weep for me the living, Antilochus, rather than for the three obols. All is lost!*[51] But what was the matter? Why did such a big crowd gather in such 395
good time?

CHREMES: Because it was resolved to put to the prytanes the following topic: The safety of the city. And first Neocleides the bleary-eyed crept forward straightaway. Then the people shouted out loudly: "O great, this man dares to address the 400
Assembly, and that, too, when the proposal concerns *safety*—
he who cannot save his own eyelid!" But he shouted out, looked around, and said: "What can I do?"

BLEPYRUS: "Ground garlic together with fig juice and throw 405
in Laconian spurge. Apply this to your eye at night."[52] That's what I'd have said had I been present.

CHREMES: After this Euaion, who's quite clever, came forward (naked or so it seemed from a distance, though of course he 410
himself said he had a cloak). Then he made a most democratic speech: "Behold, I myself need salvation to the tune of four staters.[53] Nevertheless, I'll also tell you how you'll save the city 415

---

51. In Aeschylus's lost play, *Myrmidons*, these words (for the most part) are said by Achilles to the messenger who has brought the news about Patroclus's death, except that Aristophanes substitutes "the three obols" for "the dead."

52. On spurge, Rogers quotes a contemporary work (Miller and Martyn, *Gardener's Dictionary*) which states: "The juice of every species of spurge is so acrid that it corrodes and ulcerates the body wherever it is applied: so that it is never used internally" (R, 64). Cf. Praxagora's milder remedy (lines 254–55 above).

53. I.e., about the cost of a new cloak.

and the citizens. Let clothesmakers provide the needy with winter cloaks, when first the sun turns.[54] Pleurisy would never grip us. And those who have no bed or sheets will, having had
420 their after-dinner wash, go to the tanners to sleep. And if one of the tanners shuts the door on them during the winter, he will owe three blankets."

BLEPYRUS: By Dionysus, that was a good speech. And if he added this, no one would vote against him: "The barley sellers
425 shall give three quarts to all the poor for dinner, or suffer greatly, in which case the poor would get this benefit from Nausicydes."[55]

CHREMES: Well, after this, some good-looking young man—
430 pale, like Nicias—sprang to his feet to address the Assembly, and set to work to tell us that the city should be handed over to the women. Then, the crowd of shoemakers cheered and shouted that this was well said. But those from the country grumbled loudly.

BLEPYRUS: For they have sense, by Zeus.

CHREMES: But they were fewer in number, and he was able to
435 shout them down, and he said only good things about women, and only bad things about you.

---

54. I.e., at the winter solstice (December 21).
55. "Socrates [in Xenophon's *Memorabilia* II.7] observes that Nausicydes had amassed such a fortune from his dealings in grain . . . that he became one of the wealthiest men in Athens, and had frequently to undertake, at his own expense, some of those onerous public duties which were known as λειτουργίαι [liturgies]" (R, 66).

BLEPYRUS: What did he say?

CHREMES: First he said you were a villain.

BLEPYRUS: And what about you?

CHREMES: Don't speak yet. Then he said you were a thief.

BLEPYRUS: Only me?

CHREMES: And, by Zeus, an informer as well.

BLEPYRUS: Only me?

CHREMES [pointing toward the audience]: And, by Zeus, this   440
crowd here.

BLEPYRUS: Who would say otherwise?

CHREMES: And he said a woman is a thing stuffed with intel-
ligence and moneymaking. And he said they don't at any time
divulge the secrets of the Thesmophoria, whereas you and I
always do this when serving as members of the Council.

BLEPYRUS: By Hermes, about this, at least, he told no lie.   445

CHREMES: Next he said that women lend each other cloaks,
gold, money, and drinking cups all alone, not only in the presence of witnesses, and they give it all back and they don't   450
steal, whereas most of us, he said, do.

71

BLEPYRUS: Yes, by Poseidon, even in the presence of witnesses.

CHREMES: They don't act as informers or take people to court or work to put down the democracy; but they do much that is good. And for many other things he praised the women.

455 BLEPYRUS: But what did they decide?

CHREMES: To turn the city over to them, for it seems that this is the only thing that has not been tried in the city.

BLEPYRUS: And was this agreed to?

CHREMES: I'll say.

BLEPYRUS: All the duties that the male citizens took care of are to go to the women?

CHREMES: That's the situation.

460 BLEPYRUS: So I don't go to court any more, my wife does?

CHREMES: And you'll no longer support your dependents, your wife will.

BLEPYRUS: It's no longer my business to groan at dawn?

CHREMES: By Zeus, no. That's your wife's business now. You stay home farting, without a groan.

BLEPYRUS: But here's the danger to men of our age: when the 465
women take over the reins of the city they might by force
compel us—

CHREMES: To do what?

BLEPYRUS: To fuck them.

CHREMES: But what if we're unable?

BLEPYRUS: Then they won't give us breakfast.

CHREMES: By Zeus, arrange it so that you eat breakfast and 470
fuck at the same time.

BLEPYRUS: It's no fun when they make you do it.

CHREMES: But if this benefits the city, all men must do it.

BLEPYRUS: There is an old story that the foolish and stupid 475
things we plan will all benefit us the most.

CHREMES: And may this benefit us now, O Pallas Athena and
all the gods. But I am going. Farewell.

BLEPYRUS: You too, Chremes.

Chremes and Blepyrus go into their respective houses. A few
moments later the Chorus enters cautiously. By now it is light
out, past dawn.

480 CHORUS LEADER: Advance, Chorus. Is one of the men following us? Turn around, look, guard yourself securely in case
someone from behind is watching your figure (for many are
the villains).

STROPHE:

Act like men—I think you know what to do.
485 The shame'll be great if your husbands catch you.
Wrap your cloaks around you tight,
Look all around, and to your right,
Come on, make haste, move much faster,
490 Lest our scheme end in disaster.
We're close now to the place where we began—
The house of the one who devised this plan.

ANTISTROPHE:

Now, each of you, pull the beard off your chin
495 Lest someone sees us and turns us in.
Duck into the shadow, come on, make haste,
Put your own clothes on, not a second to waste.
Hurry up, don't delay, for we can see
500 Our leader returning from the Assembly.
Hurry up, pull off your beards, course and rough,
For they have been on your jaws long enough.

Praxagora enters.

505 PRAXAGORA: O ladies, our plans have been pulled off successfully. But as swiftly as possible, before one of the men sees
us, throw off your winter cloaks, get rid of your shoes—[in a

tragic tone] *Loosen the bindings of your Laconian reins*[56]—let fall your walking sticks. [To the Chorus Leader] And you, see to all of this, as I wish to sneak inside before my husband sees me and return his cloak to where I found it, as well as anything 510 else I carried off. [Praxagora watches as the women in the chorus do what they were told.]

CHORUS LEADER: We have laid down everything you asked us to. Your only other task is to instruct us to do what seems 515 to you to be beneficial, so that we will serve you properly. For I know I have come across no woman more clever than you.

PRAXAGORA: In that case stand by me, since in the office to which I was just now elected I will need all of you as councilors. For in the Assembly, among the cheers and the shouts, you were very manly.

The Chorus exits. Praxagora is about to go into her house when Blepyrus comes out and confronts her.

BLEPYRUS: You there, Praxagora, where are you coming from? 520

PRAXAGORA: And what, dear, is that to you?

BLEPYRUS: What's it to me? How silly.

---

56. This line is probably "a quotation from Euripides or some other tragic poet, which in the original was a direction to some charioteer to let loose the Spartan reins, and give the horse its head, but is here diverted into a pompous description of the shoelatchets with which the 'red Laconians' were tied" (R, 76).

PRAXAGORA: It's not, at any rate, from a lover, as you will claim.

BLEPYRUS: Perhaps not from just one.

PRAXAGORA: But it's possible for you to test this.

BLEPYRUS: How?

PRAXAGORA: If my hair smells of perfume.

525 **BLEPYRUS:** What? Can't a woman be fucked without perfume?

PRAXAGORA: I for one cannot, I'm sad to say.[57]

BLEPYRUS: So why did you slip out quietly at dawn, taking my cloak?

PRAXAGORA: At night, some woman—a companion and friend—had labor pains and sent for me.

530 **BLEPYRUS:** What, you couldn't tell me you were going?

PRAXAGORA: And not take thought of the one who was bedridden in such a way, O husband?

BLEPYRUS: You could've at least told me. Something's wrong there.

---

57. Perhaps because of Blepyrus's odor.

PRAXAGORA: By the two gods, I went off just as I was. The one who came for me begged me to go at all costs.

BLEPYRUS: In that case, shouldn't you have taken your own 535 cloak? Instead you strip me, throw your wrap around me, and go off, leaving me there laid out like a corpse, only without a wreath or a bottle of oil.[58]

PRAXAGORA: It was cold, and I am delicate and weak, thus I 540 put this around me so that I would be warm. And I left you lying in warmth and covers, dear husband.

BLEPYRUS: But why did my Laconian shoes and my walking stick go off with you?

PRAXAGORA: In order to save your cloak, I switched shoes 545 and mimicked you, stomping my feet and striking the stones with your walking stick.[59]

BLEPYRUS: Do you know you've lost me eight quarts of wheat, which I would definitely have received from the Assembly?[60]

---

58. "This laying out . . . usually took place on the day preceding the day of the burial. The body was placed on a bier or bed, clothed in white, crowned with wreaths, and with its feet towards the door. Beside it were placed several of those small vases or bottles of oil, λήκυθοι, which were in such constant request during an Athenian's life—in the house, at the bath, in the gymnasium, and even on the battlefield; and which were finally buried with him in his grave. These funeral λήκυθοι are again mentioned infra 996, 1032, 1101, 1111" (R, 79–80).

59. She did these things, she claims, to save his cloak from clothes thieves. Assaults at night were not uncommon in Athens.

60. The eight quarts he could have purchased with the three obols pay.

PRAXAGORA: Don't worry about it, for she gave birth to a *boy*.

550 **BLEPYRUS:** The Assembly?

PRAXAGORA: By Zeus, no, the woman I went to. But has it commenced?

BLEPYRUS: Yes, by Zeus. Don't you remember me telling you yesterday?

PRAXAGORA: I'm only just now remembering.

BLEPYRUS: Do you know the decisions?

PRAXAGORA: Not I, by Zeus.

Around this time, Chremes comes out of his house and stands by, listening to their conversation.

555 **BLEPYRUS:** Then sit down and chew cuttlefish.[61] They say that the city has been handed over to *you women*!

PRAXAGORA: To do what? To weave?

BLEPYRUS: No, by Zeus, to rule.

PRAXAGORA: To rule what?

---

61. Cuttlefish is rather rubbery, and takes a long time to chew sufficiently. Perhaps this was an expression meaning "sit down and shut up." See U, 151–52, for some other interpretations.

BLEPYRUS: One and all of the affairs of the city.

PRAXAGORA: By Aphrodite, the city will indeed be blessed hereafter.

BLEPYRUS: How so?

PRAXAGORA: For many reasons. For hereafter shameful 560 actions will no longer be done by bold men: Nowhere will there be false witnessing, no more informing—

BLEPYRUS [interrupting]: For god's sake, don't do that. Don't take away my livelihood completely.

CHREMES [joining the conversation]: My fortunate man, let the lady speak.

PRAXAGORA: No theft of clothes, no envy among neighbors, 565 no being naked or poor any more, no quarreling, no seizing of goods to force payment of a debt.

BLEPYRUS: By Poseidon, this is great if she's not lying.

PRAXAGORA [addressing Chremes]: But I'll present evidence for this, so that you will bear witness in support of me, and so 570 that even this man [pointing to Blepyrus] will not speak against me.

Gradually, the Chorus has returned, the women now dressed as themselves. They gather around Praxagora.

CHORUS [to Praxagora]:

Awaken your mind, wise and shrewd,
And speak for all of us women.
Your tongue alone can describe the goods
575 We all will soon be sharing in.
Our city sorely needs some wise, new scheme,
So show what you'll do for the citizen.

[Referring to the audience:]

But say only what hasn't been said before,
580 They hate what is old—they find it a bore.
Start at once, for every delay they abhor.

PRAXAGORA: Well then, I will tell you what I believe is best.
585 But this is what I'm afraid of most of all: whether the audience
will want me to break new ground and not continue on with
things as they are.

BLEPYRUS: Don't fear breaking ground, for to us, to do this—
to neglect what is old—is preferable to every other principle.

PRAXAGORA: Now none of you answer or interrupt before you
590 understand the plan and hear the one who explains it. I assert
that it is necessary for everyone to share and have everything
in common and to live the same, and not for one to be rich
while another is miserable, nor one to farm much land while
to another there isn't enough to bury himself, nor to possess
many slaves while another doesn't even possess an attendant.
But I make one way of life common to all, and this is the same.

BLEPYRUS: How will it be common to all?   595

PRAXAGORA: You'd even eat dung before me.[62]

BLEPYRUS: Will we have the dung in common?

PRAXAGORA: By Zeus, you anticipate me with your interruption, for I was about to tell you this. First I'll make the land common for all and the silver and anything else that is held individually. Then, from these common things we will main- 600
tain you, dispensing and saving and attending to you.

CHREMES: How, if one of us does not possess land, but silver and Darics—hidden wealth?[63]

PRAXAGORA: He will lay it down for anyone to use, and he will be a perjurer if he doesn't lay it down.

BLEPYRUS: But it's through perjury that he acquired it.

PRAXAGORA: But it will be entirely of no use to him.

BLEPYRUS: How so?

---

62. "This is not (I think) abusive, or a threat, but simply the statement of a fact: 'you're very keen to anticipate', she tells him, 'even if I eat dung you'll be before me' (a case where few others would rush in)" (U, 158). (Rogers does not translate these scatological lines.)

63. "The silver of Laureium and the gold of Persia. The Darics are the famous gold coins of the Persian empire. . . ." As for 'hidden wealth', this is "a legal term, signifying movable property, as contrasted with lands and houses . . ." (R, 90–91).

605 **PRAXAGORA:** No one will do anything because of poverty, for everyone will have everything: cakes, slices of salt fish, barley loaves, clothing, wine, garlands, and chickpeas. So what would be the advantage in not laying down what he has? If you find out what it is, explain it to me.

BLEPYRUS: But nowadays, isn't it those who steal the most who live like this?

PRAXAGORA: Earlier, yes, my friend, when we used the earlier
610 laws. But now that life will be common, what is the advantage in not laying down what you have?

BLEPYRUS: If a man, seeing a girl, lusts after her and wants to playfully poke her, he'll be able to offer her only something simple when he sleeps with her, having only a share of the common property.

PRAXAGORA: But he'll be able to sleep with her free of charge. For I'm making women common to men to lie with, and to
615 make children with (for those who want to).

BLEPYRUS: Then won't everyone go after the one who is in fullest bloom, and seek to plant himself in her?

PRAXAGORA: The sorriest and most snub-nosed girls will sit down beside the majestic ones, and if he lusts after the latter, he must first bang the ugly one.[64]

---

64. Aristophanes seems to have in mind both the best- and worst-looking women *and* the highest- and lowest-class women.

BLEPYRUS: But what about us old men? If we have to have sex with the ugly women first, won't our cocks run dry before we reach the ones you spoke of? 620

PRAXAGORA: They won't fight over *you*. Take courage, don't fear, they won't fight.

BLEPYRUS: What do you mean, "over you"?

PRAXAGORA: Over your not sleeping with them. And such is your natural condition.[65]

BLEPYRUS: This makes some sense for you women, since it is decreed that no hole will be empty, but what will it do for the men? For women will run away from the ugly and go to the beautiful. 625

PRAXAGORA: But the sorriest men will keep an eye on the most handsome ones when they go out after dinner, and watch them at public places. And it won't be possible for the women to sleep with the beautiful and well-built men until they grant their favors to the ugly and small ones.

BLEPYRUS: So Lysicrates' nose will now be considered equal to the beautiful ones? 630

PRAXAGORA: By Apollo, the proposal is democratic, and it will be a great mockery of the most majestic and of those

---

65. I.e., not to be fought over for sex or to run dry (i.e., be impotent) or both.

wearing signet rings, when someone wearing ordinary shoes will say to their face, "Step aside and wait until I finish up and allow you the second pressing."[66]

635 BLEPYRUS: Then how will each of us be able to distinguish his own child?

PRAXAGORA: What's the need? Everyone will consider their fathers to be all the men who are older than they are (within a certain range of time).

BLEPYRUS: Thus they will, in good and orderly fashion, choke
640 all the old men through ignorance, since now they choke their fathers when they are known. What when they are unknown? What will stop them from even pissing on the old men?

PRAXAGORA: But the bystander won't permit it. Before, no one cared about who struck the fathers of others. But now, if someone hears a blow, fearing that the person is striking the very man who is his father, he'll fight the person who is doing this.

BLEPYRUS: You say none of these things clumsily, but if Epi-
645 curus or Leucolophus come forward calling me "papa"—this is even terrible to hear.[67]

---

66. Wine or olive oil from the second pressing is of inferior quality.

67. Some attempts have been made to identify these two men, but all we can say with any certainty is that they (or perhaps their fathers) were undesirable types.

PRAXAGORA: There is something much more terrible than this action.

BLEPYRUS: What?

PRAXAGORA: If Aristyllus, claiming to be your father, kissed you.

BLEPYRUS [horrified]: I would wail and shriek!

PRAXAGORA: At least you would smell of mint.[68] But he was born earlier, before the decree came about, so there is no 650 reason to fear that he will kiss you.

BLEPYRUS: He would have suffered for it.

CHREMES: But who will farm the land?

PRAXAGORA: The slaves. They will see to it that you, anointed in oil, move on to dinner when the shadow is ten feet long.[69]

BLEPYRUS: But what about our cloaks, what will become of them? This has to be asked.

---

68. I.e., excre-mint. This joke is based on the fact that the word for mint (καλαμίνθη) is very similar to a word for dung (μίνθος).

Aristyllus was a famous fellator who (given the nature of the joke) must have also engaged in other sexual acts with men. He thus had a kiss that Blepyrus was anxious to avoid. (See H, 386–87.) Cf. *Wealth* 314.

69. A little before sundown.

PRAXAGORA: The present ones belong to you, and we will weave you the future ones.

655 BLEPYRUS: One more question. If someone were to lose a case before the Archons[70] and was thereby fined, from what source could he pay this? For paying the fine from the common funds is not just.

PRAXAGORA: Above all, there will be no court cases!

BLEPYRUS: This remark will ruin you.

CHREMES: And I support this judgment.

PRAXAGORA: On account of what, dear, will there be court cases?

660 BLEPYRUS: For many reasons, by Apollo, but primarily for one, of course: If someone owes money but denies it.

PRAXAGORA: But from what source does the money lender lend money, if it is held in common by all? Of course, he's clearly a thief.

CHREMES: By Demeter, you demonstrate your point well.

BLEPYRUS: Then let her tell me this: In the case of assault, where men strike others, from what source will they pay a fine,

---

70. The senior political officials in Athens. They had many different functions.

when, having been well fed, they commit outrages? This, I think, will stump you.

PRAXAGORA: They will pay from the bread they eat. Whenever 665 someone takes away from their food, they'll not commit outrages again so lightly, having been punished through the stomach.

BLEPYRUS: Will no one be a thief?

PRAXAGORA: How can a person steal what he has a share in?

BLEPYRUS: Won't thieves strip off our clothes during the night?

PRAXAGORA: Not if you sleep at home, nor even if you're out-doors, as before. For sustenance belongs to all. But if someone 670 tries to strip off another's clothes, he'll give it of his own accord.[71] Why should he fight? For each person who goes to the common store will recover one better than that.

BLEPYRUS: And men won't throw dice?

PRAXAGORA: Why would one do this?

BLEPYRUS: What way of life are you making for us?

PRAXAGORA: One common to all. I assert that I shall make the town one habitation by breaking it down into one for all, so that everyone will walk among one another.

---

71. Cf. Matthew 5:40: "And if any man will sue thee at the law, and take away thy coat, let him have thy cloak also."

675 BLEPYRUS: But where will the dinner be laid out?

PRAXAGORA: I will make all law courts and public buildings into dining halls.

BLEPYRUS: How will you use the speakers' platforms in the law courts?[72]

PRAXAGORA: I'll place bowls of wine and water on them, and
680 there the children will be able to recite the deeds of the brave in war, and anyone who was cowardly and feels disgraced, will not go to dinner.

BLEPYRUS: By Apollo, that's fine! But what will you turn the balloting booths into?

PRAXAGORA: I'll set them down in the marketplace, and then, standing beside Harmodius,[73] I will make everyone draw lots, until I see each person receive their lot, rejoice, and go
685 to dine in the hall marked with whatever letter they've been assigned. The herald will summon those from the B group to go to the Best public building to dine, and those from the C

---

72. The platforms on which the participants in a lawsuit were seated.

73. N. G. L. Hammond, A History of Greece to 322 B.C., 3d ed. (Oxford: Clarendon Press, 1986), writes: "A stirring event occurred at the Panathenaic festival of the year 514—the assassination of Hipparchus by Harmodius and Aristogeiton, whose motives were personal and not political. These two 'tyrannicides' became thereafter the symbol of liberty to the Athenian people" (p. 184). Praxagora will stand "beside the saviour of Athens . . . to mark its new salvation through the women" (U, 172).

group to the one next to that, and those from the G group to the Grain-store to make room.

BLEPYRUS: So as to gulp down their food?[74]

PRAXAGORA: No, by Zeus, to dine there.

BLEPYRUS: But whoever doesn't draw a letter to dine—all these men will be expelled.

PRAXAGORA: It won't be this way with us.[75] We'll provide 690 everything, ungrudgingly, to everyone, so that drunken, with garlands and all, every single person will go away holding his torch. But the women down the road, waylaying the men coming from dinner, will say: "Come here, to our place, where 695 there's a girl in bloom." "But here with me," some other will say from an upper story, "is the most beautiful and fairest girl. However, you must lie down with me before you lie down with 700 her." And following after the good-looking youths, the sorrier

---

74. Praxagora actually mentions a β group (that will go to the στοιὰν . . . βασίλειον, the building of the King Archon), a θ group, and a κ group. There is then a joke based on the similarity between τοῦ κάππ' ("from the kappa group") and ἵνα κάπτωσιν ("so as to gulp down").

75. "It frequently happened that the state of business did not require that all the ten courts should sit: and on these occasions some of the ten dicastic sections must have drawn blanks, that is, tickets inscribed with no letter. Blepyrus supposes that in like manner some of the citizens will still draw blanks; and not unnaturally, since it would be impossible in these halls to accommodate all the 30,000 Athenian citizens. But of course a Utopia does not trouble itself about such trifles as these; and Praxagora assures him that every citizen will get a ticket, and, by means of the ticket, a dinner" (R, 110–11).

men will say: "Hey there, where are *you* going? You'll do
705 absolutely nothing when you get there! For the vote has been
given to the snubbed-nose and the ugly to fuck first, while you
in the meantime, grabbing the leaves of the two-figged
branch, have to play with yourselves outside the doorway."[76]
710 Come now, tell me, does this please you two?

BLEPYRUS: Certainly.

PRAXAGORA: In that case, then, I must go to the marketplace
(taking some loud-voiced heraldess with me), so that I may
715 receive the incoming goods. I must do this, for I've been
chosen to rule and to establish the public mess, so that you
may have your first feast today.

BLEPYRUS: We're already going to feast?

PRAXAGORA: That's what I said. And next I want to put an
end to the prostitutes, every single one of them.

BLEPYRUS: Why?

720 PRAXAGORA: It's clear. So that these ladies [she points to the
chorus] may have the primes of the young men.[77] And those

---

76. Clearly the "two-figged branch" refers to the penis and two tes-
ticles. Also significant is the mention of the doorway, which in Aristophanic comedy often stands for the vagina. (See H, 140–41.)

77. "The unusual use of the plural [τὰς ἀκμάς, the primes] gives
away the pun by disrupting the usual metaphorical connotation 'youthful
prime' expressed by the singular, emphasizing instead the literal, and thus
comical, image of 'tip,' 'point' or 'excrescence' " (H, 14).

slave-women ought not make themselves beautiful and snatch away the Cypris[78] of the free men; rather they ought to sleep only with other slaves, their piggies plucked like a goat skin.[79]

BLEPYRUS: Lead on. I'm following close behind you, so that 725 I'll be looked upon and others will say of me: "Do you not marvel at the husband of the leader?"

CHREMES: And I'll get my property ready and review it so that I can carry my goods to the marketplace.

Praxagora, Blepyrus, and the Chorus exit the stage.[80]

SCENE TWO

Chremes is in front of his house. The door is open. Helped by two slaves (Parmenon and Sicon), he is busy arranging and inspecting his things.

---

78. Cypris is another name for Aphrodite, which of course means "sex" here.

79. Henderson writes: "A pink, hairless state could . . . be achieved . . . by depilation, a practice especially associated with hetaerae and other female sex-objects. . . . Prostitutes, for whom a depilated femininity was a professional necessity, were called χοιροπῶλαι, piggie-merchants" (111). But here the meaning is most likely "plucked in the manner fitting slaves, i.e., not at all" (hence the mention of a goat-skin). (See R, 114, and U, 177.)

80. Some scholars mark a chorus (now lost) between this line and the next.

91

730 **CHREMES:** Come you here, my sieve, beautifully beautiful, first
of my things to go out the door. You've been powdered so that
you may be my basket-bearer. Indeed you have turned many of
my sacks upside down.[81] Where is the chair-bearer? Come out
735 here, pot. By Zeus but you're black. You couldn't be blacker if
you boiled the dye with which Lysicrates blackens himself.[82]
Stand alongside her. Come here, lady's maid. Bear the pitcher
here, pitcher-bearer. And you there, musician, come out, you
740 who have often roused me to go to the Assembly at the wrong
time—while it's still night!—on account of your daybreak song.[83]
[Addressing a slave who is inside his house.] You with the bowl,
come forward; bring the honeycomb, set the olive branches
745 down next to it, and bring out the tripods and the bottle of oil.
Leave the small pots and the many other pieces for now.

**The Man (from the house on the left) walks by, speaking to
himself at first.**

MAN:[84] Shall I turn in my things? I should then be an unfortunate man with a small mind. Never, by Poseidon. First I
750 shall test the situation thoroughly and see how it goes. For I'll

81. This is a parody of the Panathenaic procession. The first item (a
sieve—an ordinary household utensil) represents the beautiful maiden who
led the procession (with a basket). The maiden and sieve are similar (and
this is part of the joke) in that both are powdered—the lady for cosmetic
reasons, the sieve because many sacks of flour have passed through it.

82. Lysicrates was known for his black hair dye.

83. Ussher (179) believes Chremes most likely brings out a live
rooster to represent the processional musician.

84. There are some reasons to think that this is the unnamed man
who comes across Blepyrus in the night (at line 327 above), and I am
treating him as such.

not mindlessly throw out my sweat and thriftiness for nothing, until I find out how this whole matter stands. [To Chremes] You there, what's the meaning of all these pots and pans? Have you brought them out because you're moving, or do you bring them out to pawn them?   755

CHREMES: Absolutely not.

MAN: Why then are they lined up like this? Surely you're not sending a procession to Hiero the auctioneer?

CHREMES: By Zeus, I intend to carry off my things to the city and into the marketplace, according to the laws that were just passed.

MAN: You intend to carry them off?   760

CHREMES: Yes, certainly.

MAN: You are indeed unfortunate, by Zeus the Savior.

CHREMES: How so?

MAN: How? Easily.

CHREMES: Why? Shouldn't I obey the laws?

MAN: What laws, my poor fellow?

CHREMES: The ones that were just passed.

MAN: The ones that were just passed. What a moron you are.

765 **CHREMES:** Moron?

MAN: Well, aren't you? Surely you're the stupidest man of all time.

CHREMES: Because I do what is ordered?

MAN: Must a sensible man do what is ordered?

CHREMES: Most of all.

MAN: For a fool.

CHREMES: Don't you intend to hand in your goods?

770 **MAN:** I will be on my guard until I see what most people plan on doing.

CHREMES: What else are they doing besides getting ready to bring in their property?

MAN: I'll believe it when I see it.

CHREMES: At any rate, this is the talk in the streets.

MAN: Oh yes, talk they will.

CHREMES: And they say they will undertake to bring in their goods.

MAN: Oh yes, say they will.

CHREMES: You'll be the death of me, doubting everything.   775

MAN: Oh yes, doubt they will.

CHREMES: May Zeus destroy you.

MAN: Oh yes, destroy they will. Do you think a man among them that has a mind will bring in his goods? For giving is not something we inherited from our fathers. Instead, by Zeus, we 780 must only take, for even the gods are like that. You can tell from the hands of the statues, for whenever we pray to a god to give us good things, he stands stretching out his hand palm up, not as if to give, but to take.

CHREMES: My good man, let me do my work. [To a slave] This 785 must be tied up. Where's my strap?

MAN: You're really going to bring in your goods?

CHREMES: Yes, by Zeus, and I'm tying together these two tripods now.

MAN: Oh what folly, not waiting around for what the others will do, and then and only then—

CHREMES: Do what?

MAN: Wait longer, then waste still more time.   790

95

CHREMES: Why?

MAN: If perchance an earthquake were to occur, or lightning were to strike, or a polecat were to dart across the road, they would stop bringing in their goods, you thunderstruck idiot.

795 **CHREMES:** It would be just lovely if I were not to have a place to lay these things down.

MAN: You wouldn't find a place? Take heart, you'll be able to lay them down if you go day after tomorrow.

CHREMES: What do you mean?

MAN: I know these men vote quickly, but what they resolve to do they disavow in turn.

CHREMES: They'll bring in their goods, friend.

MAN: And if they don't, what then?

800 **CHREMES:** Don't worry, they will.

MAN: And if they don't, what then?

CHREMES: We'll fight them.

MAN: And if they're too strong, what then?

CHREMES: I'll go away and leave my goods.

MAN: And if they sell them, what then?

CHREMES: May you burst!

MAN: And if I burst, what then?

CHREMES: That would be beautiful.

MAN: You really desire to bring in your things?

CHREMES: I do. And in fact I see my neighbors bringing in 805 their goods.

MAN: Oh yes, right, Antisthenes is going to bring in his things. He'd much sooner try relieving himself for thirty days or more.[85]

CHREMES: Damn you.

MAN: But will Callimachus the chorus trainer bring in some- 810 thing?

CHREMES: More than Callias.[86]

MAN [an aside, overheard by Chremes (to whom he is referring)]: This man will throw away his substance.

---

85. See lines 366–67 above.

86. All we can say about this Callimachus is that he was probably poor. As for Callias, he was "preyed on . . . for his riches, and [his] own dissipation . . . had reduced his inheritance from two hundred talents down to barely two. . . ." (U, 188).

CHREMES: That's a rather strong way of putting it.

MAN: Strong? You speak as if you don't see such decrees constantly coming into being. Don't you know what was resolved concerning salt?[87]

815 CHREMES: I do.

MAN: And those copper coins we voted for, don't you remember that?

CHREMES: Yes, that hit me rather hard, as it turned out. For I
820 sold my grapes, took off with my jaw full of copper, and then moved along to buy barley in the market. Just when I was holding out my sack, the herald shouted that copper was not to be taken hereafter. "We use silver."

MAN: And lately, weren't we all swearing that five hundred
825 talents would be raised for the city from the 2½ percent tax that Euripides proposed? Straightaway every man was for gilding Euripides. But when the matter was well examined, and a "Corinthus, son of Zeus," appeared and it was not enough, then every man was for tarring Euripides.[88]

---

87. This is the first of three examples of the Athenians changing their minds or failing to act according to what they had decreed.

Regarding the salt: "the measure (says the scholiast) was meant to bring down the price of salt, but never put into operation" (U, 188). Nothing else is known of this.

88. "[T]he words ὁ Διὸς Κόρινθος (Corinthus, son of Zeus, the eponymous founder of Corinth) were used over and over again, by way of menace, to the revolted Megarians by the Corinthian ambassadors, till the

CHREMES: It's not the same, friend. Then *we* were ruling, now 830
the women are.

MAN: I shall watch out for them, by Poseidon, lest they piss
on me.

CHREMES: You don't realize that you speak nonsense. [To his
slave] Boy, take up the yoke.

Chremes makes the final preparations before taking his goods
away. Meanwhile the Heraldess arrives.

HERALDESS: *All* citizens (for this is the way it is now[89]). Come 835
on, hurry straight to your generaless, so that by drawing lots
fortune will tell each of you where you will dine. The tables
are prepared and heaped high with all good things, and the 840
couches are heaped with blankets and cushions. They're
mixing wine in bowls, the perfume-selling girls are standing
by, and the fish slices are being grilled. They're shoving spits
into hares and baking round cakes. Garlands are being woven 845
and desserts are being cooked. The youngest girls are boiling
pots of pea soup, and Smoius in his riding suit is among them,
licking the women's bowls clean.[90] And Geron moves along

Megarians rose up, defeated the Corinthians, and secured their own inde-
pendence. Hence the words became a proverbial expression applicable
either to wearisome iteration . . . or to grand professions which are not jus-
tified by the results, as in the present passage" (R, 129).

89. "Before this (as Rogers explains, rightly) invitations to public
banquets were an honour bestowed upon a few distinguished people . . ."
(U, 190).

90. "Bowls and dishes tend to appear in descriptions of cunnilingus.

850 wearing a dainty shawl and sandals, laughing aloud with another youngster, his shoes and threadbare cloak lying there discarded.[91] Move along to your places, as the one with the barley cakes stands ready. Open your mouths wide. [She exits.]

MAN: In that case I'll go. For why should I stay here when the city thinks it best to go?

855 CHREMES: Where will you go? You haven't turned in your property.

MAN: To the dinner.

CHREMES: You can't go until you've carried off your goods, not if these women have any sense.

MAN: But I'll bring them.

CHREMES: When?

MAN: Look, my going to dinner before I've turned in my things won't be an obstacle to them, friend.

CHREMES: Why not?

... [N]ote the presence at this banquet of the notorious cunnilinctor, Smoeus" (H, 166).

Henderson (276–77) claims that references to horses and horsemanship are frequently used to indicate "mounting and riding" of another kind.

91. "Geron ... had seemingly reached the age his name denoted [i.e., old age], but now was acting like a young lad ..." (U, 192).

MAN: I think others will bring their goods even later than I will.

CHREMES: Are you really going to dinner all the same?　860

MAN: Yes, for what else am I to do? Those with good intentions must assist the city in any way possible.

CHREMES: And if they stop you, what then?

MAN: I'll lower my head and charge them.

CHREMES: And if they whip you, what then?

MAN: I'll summon them into court.

CHREMES: And if they laugh at you, what then?

MAN: Having stationed myself at the door—　865

CHREMES: What will you do? Tell me.

MAN: I'll snatch some food as they bring it in.

CHREMES: In that case, go *after* me. [Addressing two of his slaves] You, Sicon and Parmenon, take up all my possessions.

MAN: Come now, I'll help you.

CHREMES: Absolutely not. For I fear that when I'm laying 870 down my goods beside the generaless, you'll claim them. [Chremes and his slaves exit.]

MAN: By Zeus, I need some cunning plan so that I'll keep my
875 goods *and* somehow share in these common baked goods. Yes,
I think I know what to do! I must go to where the dinner's
going to be, and I must not delay. [The Man rushes off.]

SCENE THREE[92]

Evening. Three other houses, pretty much the same as the previous three. The house on the left is occupied by the First Hag, the center house by the Girl, and the house on the right by the Second Hag. The scene begins with the First Hag peeping her head out of the upstairs window.

FIRST HAG: Why haven't the men come here? The hour for
880 it is long past. I'm standing idly by, plastered with white lead
and wearing my saffron-colored dress, humming some tune to
myself while I playfully ponder how I might capture one of the
men going by. Muses, come to my mouth and devise some
little Ionian song.

While the First Hag is speaking, a Girl appears from behind
the upstairs window of the center house.

GIRL [to the First Hag]: This time when you poked your head
885 out you did so before me, O putrid one. You thought that since
I wasn't present you might pick the unwatched grapes and

---

92. Originally there may have been a chorus between the last scene
and this one. This scene was anticipated at lines 693–709.

attract someone by singing. But if you do this, I will oppose you with song. For even though the audience finds this irritating, there is nevertheless something agreeable and comic about it.

FIRST HAG: Talk to *this*, and go away. [She makes an obscene 890 gesture.[93]] [Addressing the piper who plays for the Chorus.] But you, my dear little piper, take the pipes and play a tune worthy of me and you. [Piper begins to play. First Hag begins to sing.[94]]

If a man wants to feel something good,
Then he should lie with a woman like me, 895
Experience isn't found in immature girls,
But in real women, ripe and ready.

A girl quickly tires of her man,
To another she would soon fly away.
But mature women treat their men better,
By your side, my whole life, I would stay.

GIRL [singing]:

Oh, do not be so hard on us girls, 900
Just 'cause nature has made us so nice

---

93. "[P]ossibly she: (a) points to her *pudenda* . . . , in other words, the girl is to be left (like the youths by *their* elders, 707) to find consolation for herself, (b) tosses her an imitation penis (ὄλισβος . . .), (c) offers her posterior . . . , which is probably closer to the meaning . . ." (U, 197). Henderson seems to accept (b) at one point (6), but elsewhere suggests "this" refers to the middle finger (30, 232). Rogers (137) also accepts (b).

94. The hag and the girl duel in song (lines 893–923).

103

Aristophanes

(For softness blooms on our apples[95]
And grows on our tender young thighs.)

Whereas you, hag, it's plain to see,
Are rough from your toes to your head,
But once you're well plucked and well rubbed,[96]
905 You'll make a fitting lover—for the dead!

FIRST HAG:

Next time you want a banging
And you give your man a shout,
May you throw away your bed
And may your hole fall out.

And when you want some loving
And you're lying in your bed,
May you reach for your man
910 And grab a *snake* instead.[97]

GIRL [to herself]:

My mother's left me all alone,
It's a chance I don't want to miss.
But my lover isn't here yet—
Will I miss my chance at bliss?

---

95. In Greek, "apples" is often used to refer to breasts.
96. Perhaps when her body hair is plucked and she is well rubbed with white lead.
97. The snake refers to a limp penis (H, 90).

[Addressing the First Hag again]

But dear, I'm being rude,   915
You too deserve some bliss.
I beg you, I beseech you:
Call on Orthagoras.[98]

FIRST HAG:

Now you're one to talk, wench,
Scratching like an Ionian.[99]
You also seem to me to be
A lambda—as in Lesbian.[100]   920

You'll not snatch away my playthings
For yourself, whatever you might say.
And the time I have coming to me
You'll neither ruin nor take away.

GIRL: Sing as much as you want and keep poking your head
out like a polecat.

---

98. 'Ορθός can mean "erect" in Greek (H, 10). Ussher (202) thinks "Orthagoras" might refer to an imitation penis.

99. "The ὄλισβος [imitation penis] was Ionian." (U, 203)

100. Where I translate "as in Lesbian," the Greek actually says "in the manner of the Lesbians." Henderson (381) says the "manner of the Lesbians" is fellatio: "Like Englishmen and Americans, who attribute shameless lovemaking techniques to the gay French, the Attic poets seem to have attributed the invention and practice of fellatio to the luxurious Lesbians. . . ."

Ussher (203) thinks the reference to lambda (Λ, λ) might also stand for "the legs stretched out and wide apart."

925 **FIRST HAG:** No one will go to you before coming to me.

GIRL: Not to my funeral, at least. That's a new one, you smelly old bitch!

FIRST HAG: No, it's old.

GIRL: You're right, why would someone say what's new to an old hag?

FIRST HAG: It's not my old age that will distress you.

GIRL: Then what will, more of your rouge and white lead?

930 **FIRST HAG:** Why are you talking to me?

GIRL: Why are you poking your head out?

FIRST HAG: Me? I'm singing a song to myself—a song for Epigenes, my lover.

GIRL: You have a lover other than Geres?[101]

FIRST HAG: You'll see, for he'll be with me shortly.

The Youth enters and moves cautiously toward the Girl's house.

GIRL: Here he is himself.

---

101. I.e., Old Age.

FIRST HAG: He doesn't need anything from you, pest. 935

GIRL: Yes, by Zeus, he does, you decaying wench. He'll show you himself shortly. Meanwhile, I'll go down to him. [She disappears behind her window.]

FIRST HAG [remaining for a time at her window]: I will, too, so that you'll know that I understand much more than you do.

YOUTH [who has seen the Girl and the First Hag and has heard the end of their conversation, to himself]: Would that it were possible to lie with my girl, and that it wasn't neces- 940 sary to bang a snubbed-nose old woman before that, for this is unbearable to a free man.

FIRST HAG [to herself]: In sorrow, then, will you bang me, by Zeus. For this is not the time of Charixena.[102] According to 945 the law this is just, if we are to live democratically. But I'll go and watch what you're going to do. [She leaves her window.]

YOUTH: O gods, would that I might catch my fair one alone, to whom I go drunk with desire.

GIRL [reappearing at her window]: I deceived that abom- 950 inable old hag. For she's gone, thinking that I'm staying

---

102. Charixena, a "musician and composer of erotica . . . , had possibly persisted in efforts to attract—despite her age—and thus become a byword" (U, 209).

indoors. But here's the very man we were talking about. [**She begins to sing.**[103]]

Come here, come here,
My dear, come to me.
Advance, and this night
My bedfellow you'll be.

955 How I long for your curls—
Eros has set me on fire—
I'm overwhelmed and worn out
By some strange desire.

I beseech you, Eros,
I beg you—release me.
Get this youth into
My bed to relieve me.

YOUTH [singing]:

960 Come here, come here,
My dear, come to me.
Run down, open wide
Your door for me.

---

103. What follows is some kind of love duet. S. Douglas Olson, "The 'Love Duet' in Aristophanes' *Ecclesiazusae*," *Classical Quarterly* 38 (1988): 328–30, argues persuasively that "the poetic basis of the scene is an Aristophanic adaptation of a well-known poetic genre with exceptionally clear and prominent sexual roles, the paraclausithyron [a "song sung by an excluded lover from the street to his beloved within"]. By confusing sexual identities within this adapted song, and by at the same time assigning to the Young Man lines clearly 'intended' for the Young Woman, Aristophanes offers an elaborate poetic commentary on Praxagora's new world."

If not, I shall drop here,
Utterly neglected.
But that's not what I want,
To lie here rejected.

I *want* to be deep in your hollow,
Trading blows with your behind.   965
Why oh why, Aphrodite,
Do you drive me out of my mind?

The words I've sung to you so far
Can't express my terrible need.   970
Open up to me, dear, bid me welcome,
With the greatest possible speed.

Because of you, I sing and complain.
You, dear, are the source of this great pain.

Oh my darling, wrought with gold.
Cypris's young sprout,
Honey of the Muses,
Nursling of the Graces,
Face of Delicacy.
Open up! Bid me welcome!

Because of you, I sing and complain.   975
You, dear, are the source of this great pain.

He knocks hard and rapidly on her door.

FIRST HAG [opening her door]: Hello there, why are you
knocking? Are you looking for me?

YOUTH: Are you kidding?

FIRST HAG: And yet you banged on my door.

YOUTH: Strike me dead if I did.

FIRST HAG: What do you need then, coming here with a torch?

YOUTH: I'm searching for some Anaphlystian man.

FIRST HAG: Who?

980 YOUTH: Not Sebinus, whom you probably expect.[104]

FIRST HAG: Yes, by Aphrodite, whether you want him or not.

YOUTH [speaking in the manner of a government official]: But we're not now taking cases over sixty years old. We've postponed them till some later time. We're deciding on those cases under twenty years old.

985 FIRST HAG: That was under the previous rule, sweetie. Now it's decreed that you must take our cases first.

---

104. Anaphlystus was the name of an actual deme, but was often used in comedy because it sounds a lot like ἀναφλᾶν, a word for masturbation. Similarly, the name Sebinus would suggest the word βινεῖν (i.e., fuck), and could thus be exploited for comic purposes. The youth tells the hag she should not expect Sebinus.

YOUTH: This only applies to the man who wants to, at least according to the law in dice.[105]

FIRST HAG: You didn't *dine* according to the law in dice.

YOUTH: I don't know what you mean. But I must bang on *this* door. [He knocks again.]

FIRST HAG: When you've banged on my door first.   990

YOUTH: We don't just this moment crave a rough cloth.

FIRST HAG: I know that I am loved. It's only that you're surprised to find me at the door. Never mind all that: draw your lips near.

YOUTH: But, my dear, I fear your lover.

FIRST HAG: Who?

YOUTH: The best of painters.   995

FIRST HAG: And who is that?

YOUTH: He who paints the oil-flasks for the dead. But go away, so that he'll not see you at the door.[106]

---

105. There was probably a rule in dice that a player could take a turn or pass, depending on what he wanted.

106. "The Hag speaks as if she were a shy and modest young maiden, whom it is surprising to find out of doors alone. The youth tells her, in effect . . . , that her fittest lover is the 'undertaker,' who paints the oil-bot-

FIRST HAG: I know, I know what you want.

YOUTH: Yes, and I know what *you* want, by Zeus.

FIRST HAG: By Aphrodite, who was appointed to protect me,
1000 I'll not let you go. **[She grabs him.]**

YOUTH: You're out of your mind, old hag.

FIRST HAG: And you speak foolishly. Nevertheless, I'll take you to my bed.

YOUTH: Why do we buy hooks for drawing up buckets of water, when it's possible to lower down an old hag like this to collect the buckets from the wells?[107]

1005 FIRST HAG: Don't make fun of me, dear, come to me.

YOUTH: But I don't have to, unless you've paid the $\frac{1}{5}$ percent tax on me to the city.[108]

FIRST HAG: By Aphrodite, you most certainly must do it, as I take pleasure in sleeping with men of your age.

---

tles carried out and buried with the dead. . . . And he warns her not to be seen at the door . . . , lest the undertaker should think she is a corpse, and come to carry *her* out" (R, 151).

107. He is most likely referring to her skinny and bent hands and limbs, which look like hooks.

108. Perhaps there was an actual Athenian law such that one could not exercise his privileges as a citizen unless he had paid to the city one five-hundredth of his possessions.

YOUTH: But I am disgusted by hags of your age, and I'll never 1010
be persuaded to do it.

FIRST HAG [whipping out a document]: By Zeus, *this* will
compel you.

YOUTH: And what is *this*?

FIRST HAG: A decree according to which you must come
with me.

YOUTH: Tell me what in the world it is.

FIRST HAG: Indeed, I'm going to. "It was decreed by the 1015
women that: If a young man lusts after a girl, he cannot pound
her until he bangs a hag first. But if he does not wish to bang
her first, but lusts after the girl, let it be permissible for the
older woman to drag off the youth with impunity, grabbing 1020
him by his peg."

YOUTH: Oh, I will today become a Procrustes.[109]

FIRST HAG: You must obey our laws.

---

109. The Greek word that I have translated "bang first," προκρούειν
(which can also mean "stretch"), is very close to the name Προκρούστες.
"The name of the fabled robber, Procrustes, who stretched his victims on a
bed, puns on the obscene meaning in the joke made by the desperate young
man . . . : he is about to suffer, at the hands of the three hags, a 'pro-
crustean' torture in both senses of the word" (H, 306).

YOUTH: But what if some man, one of my friends or demesmen, should come and bail me out?

1025 FIRST HAG: Now no man has authority beyond a bushel.[110]

YOUTH: Is it not possible to decline the office on oath?[111]

FIRST HAG: You mustn't wriggle out of this.

YOUTH: I'll pretend to be a merchant.[112]

FIRST HAG: You'll regret it.

YOUTH: What then must I do?

FIRST HAG: Come with me. [She tries to drag him.]

YOUTH: And this is a necessity?

FIRST HAG: It's a Diomedean necessity.[113]

1030 YOUTH: In that case, first strew the dittany under us, and set four crushed branches of vine beneath, and decorate her with

---

110. "No man can bail you out; for no man's credit extends beyond one medimnus ['bushel'] of barley now. The contracts of women, the Scholiast tells us, were restricted by law to the value of one medimnus: now, therefore, men and women having changed places, the same limit is imposed upon the contracts of men" (R, 154–55).

111. Aristophanes has in mind "an excuse (such as ill health) put forward upon oath for the purpose of escaping some public duty" (R, 155).

112. In Athens, merchants were exempt from military service.

113. Apparently, this was a proverbial expression; cf. Plato, *Rep.* VI.493d.

114

ribbons, and set the oil bottles beside us, and set the water jug down before the door.[114]

First Hag: And you'll still buy me a garland.

Youth: Yes, by Zeus, at least if it's a wax one. For I know that 1035 in the house you'll straightaway crumble into pieces.[115]

The Girl, who has been watching from her door, now comes out and gets involved.

Girl: Where are you dragging him? [She grabs the Youth and tries to pull him toward her door.]

First Hag: This man that I'm leading home is *mine.*

Girl: That's unwise. He's not old enough to lie with you, 1040 being so young, for you would be more a mother to him than a wife. So if you women establish this law, you will fill the earth with Oedipuses.

First Hag [who lets go, revolted at what she hears]: O you disgusting girl, you invented this speech out of envy. But I'll take vengeance on you.[116] [She runs off.]

---

114. He is describing a funeral bier instead of a nuptial bed.

115. She is asking for a wedding garland, while he has in mind a wax funeral one.

116. "This aspect of the law has not struck the hag, and horrified—as well as enraged at being cheated—she runs (like Jocasta, to whom, by implication, the girl's words in 1042 compare her) back into the house in agitation . . ." (U, 220). Despite what she says, we do not see her again.

Aristophanes

1045 YOUTH [to the Girl]: By Zeus the Savior, you have done me
a favor, my dearest, setting me free from the hag. So in return
for these good deeds, tonight I'll give you a big, fat favor.

She takes his hand and pulls him toward her door. Meanwhile,
a Second Hag, who is uglier than the first, comes out of her
house (on the right).

1050 SECOND HAG [shouting at the Girl]: You there, where are you
dragging this guy, against the law, when it has been stated in
writing that he's to lie with me first? [She grabs the Youth.]

YOUTH [who recoils and backs away]: Oh, wretched me!
Where have you popped out from, you horror? This evil one
is even worse than the other one was.

SECOND HAG: Come here. [She grabs him again.]

YOUTH [to the Girl, who has had it and is going back into her
1055 house]: Don't watch while I'm being dragged by this hag, and
do nothing! I entreat you!

SECOND HAG: It's not I but the law that drags you.

YOUTH: It's not the law that drags me, but some Empusa,
clothed in a blister of blood.[117]

117. Empusa was "a bogey . . . identified with Hecate . . . in one of
her numerous disguises . . ." (U, 221).

116

SECOND HAG: Follow me, little coward, make haste and don't babble.

YOUTH: Come now, let me first go to the outhouse to gain 1060 confidence in myself. If not, you'll straightaway see me shitting myself out of fear.

SECOND HAG: Be confident, come. You'll relieve yourself inside.

YOUTH: In more ways than I want, I fear. But I'll pay bail to 1065 ensure my return.

SECOND HAG: There will be no bail in this case! [She starts to drag him with greater force.]

The Third Hag, who is by far the ugliest, enters and comes up from behind the Youth and grabs him. He does not see her at first.

THIRD HAG [to the Youth]: Where are you sneaking off to with this woman?

YOUTH [who still has not seen her]: I'm not, I'm being dragged. But whoever you are, may many goods come to you, since you didn't overlook me when I was in distress. [Turns and sees her. He is absolutely horrified.] O Heracles, O Pans, O Corybantes, O Twin Sons of Zeus, this evil is worse still.[118] 1070

118. "Now he suddenly discovers what she is, and calls for help to Heracles, the Destroyer of Monsters, and to Castor and Polydeuces, the great twin brethren, the helpers of men in peril and distress. With these he apostrophizes the Pans and the Corybantes, as authors of those panics and frenzies with which his mind is at present distracted" (R, 161).

117

But what sort of thing is this, I entreat you, whatever is this?
A monkey plastered with white lead, or a hag who has risen
from the Majority?[119]

THIRD HAG: Don't make fun of me, follow me. [She grabs
him by the arm.]

SECOND HAG [grabbing the Youth by the other arm]: No,
come *here.*

1075 THIRD HAG: I will never release you.

SECOND HAG: Nor will I.

YOUTH: You'll tear me apart, you detestable witches.

SECOND HAG: Yes, for you must obey me, according to the law.

THIRD HAG: Not if another hag, even uglier, appears.

YOUTH: If I die horribly because of you, tell me, how will I
1080 reach my beautiful girl?

THIRD HAG: That's your problem. But this you must do.

YOUTH [defeated]: Which one shall I screw first so that I'll be
set free?

SECOND HAG: Don't you know? Come here.

---

119. I.e., from the dead.

YOUTH [to the Second Hag, indicating with his head the Third Hag]: Make *this* hag release me.

THIRD HAG: Come here, to me.

YOUTH [to the Third Hag, indicating the Second]: If *she* will release me.

SECOND HAG: I won't release you, by Zeus.   1085

THIRD HAG: Nor will I.

YOUTH: You would make rough ferrymen.

SECOND HAG: Why?

YOUTH: You'd wear the passengers out by dragging them.[120]

SECOND HAG: Be quiet and come here.

THIRD HAG: By Zeus, come to me.

YOUTH: This is clearly like Cannonus's decree: I have to fuck 1090 while I'm fettered.[121] How then will I be able to row on both sides with only one oar?

---

120. "He is alluding, the Scholiast tells us, to the rough competition of the rival ferrymen, each striving to secure the passenger for his own boat . . ." (R, 163).

121. According to this decree, a person who harms the Athenian people must answer the charges against him in fetters.

119

SECOND HAG: Beautifully, if you eat down a pot of onions.[122]

YOUTH: Woe, what ill fortune. I'm being dragged and I'm already nearly to the door. [They are close to the Second Hag's door.]

1095 THIRD HAG: That won't do you any good, for I'll fall in with you.

YOUTH: No, by the gods, for it is better to embrace one evil than two.

THIRD HAG: Yes, by Hecate, whether you want to or not.

1100 YOUTH [in a tragic tone]: O thrice ill fated me, if I must fuck a putrid woman all night and all day, and then, when I am free of her, once again fuck a toad with an oil flask near her cheeks. Am I not ill fated? No, I am heavy fated, by Zeus the Savior—an unlucky man 1105 who will be shut up with these beasts. But if (as is likely) I suffer something when I sail into harbor pulled by these two whores, bury me at the very mouth of the entrance, grab the upper hag, who survives, 1110 for my grave marker, smear her with tar, then pour molten lead around her ankles and stand her up as a substitute for an oil flask.[123]

---

122. Or bulbs or truffles. These were considered an aphrodisiac.

123. Clearly the Youth did not expect to survive this ordeal, and his last words in the play read something like a will. Here is one interpretation of what he has in mind: "It would seem that as they go tumbling into the second Hag's house, the youth is sandwiched between the two; one of whom is κάτω [lower], pulling him in, and the other ἄνω [upper], trying to drag him back. The one who is [below] will . . . fall to pieces . . . ; and so will apparently form the young man's grave. The one who is [upper] will survive, but she is to be blackened with pitch, and fixed to the place with molten lead, so as to represent . . . one of the funeral [oil flasks]" (R, 167).

The scene ends with all three tumbling into the house. The door closes.

SCENE FOUR

An Athenian street at night. There is much festivity. The Chorus makes up the female half of the crowd. Someone's maid enters.

MAID: Blessed are the people, and I am happy, and my mistress is most blessed of all, and you women who are standing by the door,[124] and all our neighbors and demesmen, and besides these good people, I, the servant, who have drenched 1115 my head with perfume, dear Zeus. But far surpassing the rest are these little jars of Thasian wine.[125] For they remain in my head for a long time, while all the others wither and fly away, so they are by far the best, O gods, by far. [Addressing a non- 1120 existent servant] Mix me some unmixed wine. Choosing whatever has the best fragrance will make us merry the whole night. [To the Chorus] But tell me, women, where my master is, the husband of my mistress. 1125

CHORUS LEADER: It seems to us you'll find him if you stay here.

A few moments later, her Master enters. He seems mostly interested in the women.

---

124. The Chorus, standing near the door to one of the houses.

125. The maid may be rambling a bit because of too much wine. Thasian wine was known for its fragrance.

MAID: You're right, for here he is, going to dinner. O master, blessed and thrice fortunate.

1130 MASTER: Me?

MAID: You, by Zeus, as no other man is. For who is more fortunate than you, who alone of the more than thirty thousand citizens that make up the multitude has not been to the dinner?

CHORUS LEADER: You clearly speak of a happy man.

1135 MAID: Where are you off to?

MASTER: I'm going to the dinner.

MAID: By Aphrodite, by far the last of all. Nevertheless, my lady ordered me to lay hold of you and lead you and the girls
1140 with you to dinner. Some Chian wine[126] is left over, and the other good things, too. Don't delay in going. And if any in the audiences happens to think well of the play, and if any of the judges is not looking elsewhere,[127] come with us, for we'll give everything.

1145 MASTER: Won't you ask *all* of them, like a lady, and leave no one aside, but freely invite old men, young men, and little boys? The

---

126. The best and most expensive of wines.

127. I.e., if any of the judges does not favor Aristophanes' rival playwrights (U, 231).

128. This play was performed in competition with four others, the order of performance determined by lot. It is not known how well the play did.

dinner is ready for all of them—if they go home. But I'll hurry 1150
off to the dinner now. Fortunately I have this torch here.

CHORUS LEADER: Why, since you have a torch, do you waste
time instead of taking these girls and leading them to the
dinner? And in the time you are going down to dinner, I shall
sing you a dinner song. But first I want to make a small sug- 1155
gestion to the judges: To the wise ones, remember to judge me
victor for my wisdom, while to the ones who laugh pleasantly,
remember to judge me victor because of the laughter (thus I
am clearly urging nearly all of you to judge me victor); and
remember that it was my lot and not because of me that I went 1160
first.[128] Remembering all these things you must not swear
falsely, but always judge the plays fairly and not like evil courtesans, who always remember only their very last men. Oh,
oh, it's time, dear Women, if we intend to do this thing, to 1165
swing and to sway to the dinner. So move your feet in Cretan
fashion[129] **[to the Master]**—and you too.

MASTER: I'll do it.

CHORUS LEADER: Now these agile girls <must go to the
dinner, following>[130] the rhythm with their legs. For soon
there will be. . . .

---

128. This play was performed in competition with four others, the order
of performance determined by lot. It is unknown how well the play did.

129. Perhaps after the fashion of a Cretan dance in which the leg is
raised (see R, 234).

130. Ussher and others mark a lacuna here (lines 1166–67) which I
fill in briefly and simply, not following any of the many clever conjectures
(see, for example, Ussher's apparatus).

Aristophanes

The Chorus joins in, singing and dancing with the Master.

1170 Saltfishanmusselsandogfishanshark-
Oilanpicklinganhoneyanbrine-
Pigeonanblackbirdancock'sbrainanlark-
1175 Wagtailanrabbitanwingsinnewwine.[131]

They stop dancing.

CHORUS LEADER [to the Master]:

So now that you have heard this,
Quick and quickly grab a bowl,
Then get yourself some porridge,[132]
For they're stuffin' 't down their throats.

They resume their dancing.

1180 Now kick your legs up,
Hurrah, hurrah.
We're off to dinner,
Hurrah, hurrah.
On to victory,
Hurrah, hurrah,
Hip, hip, hurrah.

---

131. As far as I know, this is the longest word in Western literature.
This dish may be the perfect symbol of Praxagora's communism: different meals (both delicacies and common fare) have been mixed together to become one common meal with a view to the satisfaction of bodily pleasure.
132. This is most likely another contrary-to-expectation joke. We expect the Master to be fed the grand meal, not porridge.

Titles in Prometheus's Literary Classics Series

TITLE	PRICE	QUANTITY
Henry Adams—*Esther*	$ 9.95	_____
Aristophanes—*Assembly of Women* (*Ecclesiazusae*) (Translated with an introduction by Robert Mayhew)	8.95	_____
Anton Chekov—*Stories of Men* (Translated by Paula Ross)	13.95	_____
Anton Chekov—*Stories of Women* (Translated by Paula Ross)	16.95	_____
Kate Chopin—*The Awakening*	6.95	_____
Stephen Crane—*Maggie: A Girl of the Streets*	5.95	_____
Nathaniel Hawthorne—*The Scarlet Letter*	6.95	_____
Henry James—*The Turn of the Screw* and *The Lesson of the Master*	6.95	_____
Sinclair Lewis—*Main Street*	8.95	_____
Herman Melville—*The Confidence Man*	8.95	_____
John Neal—*Rachel Dyer*	6.95	_____
Edgar Allan Poe—*Eureka: A Prose Poem*	7.95	_____
Mark Twain—*The Mysterious Stranger*	5.95	_____
Walt Whitman—*Leaves of Grass*	8.95	_____
	TOTAL	_____

(Prices subject to change without notice.)

Phone Orders (24 hours):
Toll free (800) 421–0351 • FAX (716) 691–0137
Email: PBooks6205@aol.com

Ship to: _____

Address _____

_____

City _____

County (*N.Y. State Only*) _____

Telephone _____

Prometheus Acct. # _____

❑ Payment enclosed (or)

Charge to ❑ VISA ❑ MasterCard

A/C: ❑❑❑❑❑❑❑❑❑❑❑❑❑❑❑❑❑❑❑❑❑❑

Exp. Date _____ / _____

Signature _____